Ancient Mountain People

Dr. F. Fleischer

Ancient Mountain People

by

Dr. F. Fleischer

New Millennium
310 Kennington Road, London SE11 4LD.

Copyright © 1996 Dr. F. Fleischer

All rights reserved. No part of this publication
may be reproduced in any form, except for
the purposes of review, without prior
written permission from the
copyright owner.

Printed and bound by B.W.D. Ltd. Northolt, Middx.
Issued by New Millennium*
ISBN 1 85845 047 0
*An imprint of The Professional Authors' & Publishers' Association

Contents

	Page
Kashmir	1
Ladakh	21
Mexico	47
Lima	111

Illustrations

	Page
Map of Srinagar	7
'Home Sweet Home'	8
'Shikara', watertaxi	11
'Quash' on the floating market	12
'Stupa'	20
Lamayura village	25
Shey Gompa	30
Fields of Tikse Gompa	31
Ladakhian farmer	32
Our Host's wife in Leh	38
View of Mexico City	56
Olmec sculpture	57
House of the Wise Man	83
Corbel Arch	84
Chaak-Mol	85
Caracol	92
Cathedral of Guernavaca	97
Atlantas	100
Lima Cathedral	120
Pyramid of the Moon	121
Chimu sculpture	122
Placa da Armas	128
Machu Picchu	136
Floating island of the Urus Indians	152
La Compania de Jesu	161
Petroglyps	162

Kashmir
September 1977

Once again I am starting to write this on a grey and dreary Sunday evening, hoping to recapture the joy and excitement of our venture to Kashmir and further on to 'Little Tibet'. It was already an adventure to prepare for the trip, to borrow a kit-bag, water-bottle and sleeping bag for our journey to the Himalayas.

Arriving at London Airport, we looked for passengers equally equipped for life under canvas. We soon found one woman, guarding a mountain of gear. Her own, as well as that of one of the men, who had drifted off. We met the leader of our party. Suddenly a tall, white-haired lady bore down upon me. Fixing me with her piercing blue eyes, she announced: "I am Barbara W., the journalist. Who are you?"

Once we had arrived in the departure lounge, we were informed that the Geographical Magazine, which was on sale in the shop, carried an article about Ladakh. We all rushed to get a copy and avidly read the story. We had not been able to find much information about this remote corner of India before our trip.

The journey was long but comfortable. We sat next to our tour leader, a well-known botanist who specialised in the flora of the Himalayas. He was half Russian. We talked, read, ate and slept. We saw the flames of the oil refineries piercing the velvet sky when we touched down at Muscat. Daylight broke. Eventually we landed at Delhi Airport. It was incredibly sticky and hot. We were served breakfast in a somewhat disorganised fashion in a small restaurant overlooking the airfield. Here, Rebecca joined us. She was an Israeli, who proved to be one of the most kindly and generous young women I ever met. She had no inhibitions, was completely relaxed and smoked non stop. She was a married woman, her husband was English. They now live with their two little girls on a kibbutz near the Lebanese frontier. For the last two years the family had lived in London, engaged in community work. The children voted to go straight back home, whilst the parents proceeded to Delhi. Rebecca joined us for the rest of the trip whilst her husband took part in a climbing expedition to explore the wild mountains of Nepal.

Once again we had to wait. It was tedious, since Delhi Airport, judged by our standards, was primitive, with little to offer apart from Mrs. Ghandi's continuous exhortations on the television screens and her ever-present slogans displayed on the walls. We stepped outside the airport into the brilliant sunshine and noticed the sacred pale cows grazing contentedly amongst cars and bicycles which were parked there. Eventually a saried lady told us the reason for the delay. A German plane had been hijacked to Pakistan and now the plane which was to convey us to Srinagar had been commandeered to bring back the released hostages. We watched the plane arriving and saw the freed hostages walk across the tarmac. Finally we were airborne again. It was evening when we touched down in Srinagar. Taxis were waiting for us to drive us swiftly to Dal Lake. It is a beautiful lake and looked very romantic with the mist rising over its stillness. The water taxi, the Shikara, awaited us at the bottom of the landing quay as our cars drew up along the lakeside. We stepped into this fairy craft, lightly guided by the boat boy, and reclined dreamily on the soft cushions whilst the boat glided across to the landing stage, which was garlanded with flowers ready to receive us on the famous houseboats. These were flat-bottomed craft, fashioned like the Oxford boats. In former days local laws forbade non-Indians from buying houses or grounds. The British built these houseboats to spend their leave and leisure up in the cooler air of Kashmir on the pleasant waters of the lake. These boats were now used for tourists. They were pure Victoriana, elaborately carved, with a small porch leading into the sitting room. This was fully furnished with carpets, chandeliers, plush covered easychairs. Next to it was our dining room with the galley adjoining. Three double bedrooms, each with their own bathroom, completed our cosy accommodation.

Ahmed was in charge. In his pyjamas, head covered as becomes a good Muslim and barefooted, he appeared to see and hear everything. We called him 'Charlie Chaplin of the East' since, with his little black moustache, his comic expression and his straight-faced humour, he reminded us strongly of the famous clown. Deftly he served us, anticipating our every need. The table was adorned with flowers and the napkins were most artistically arranged in a different pattern at each meal. He huddled in his Kashmiri blanket on the porch awaiting our return in the evenings when we called on the rest of our party in their own houseboats. One was called Acropolis, pronounced 'Acro Palace' by the locals. Once we had retired to our rooms, Ahmed came and slept in one corner of our drawing room. It was he who decided which of the many traders were permitted to come aboard. He reigned supreme, ably assisted by a tousle-haired youth. The cooking was done at 'the back side, madam', as he put it when asked. Actually each houseboat had a kitchen in tow, tucked discreetly away at the back. Meals were seriously discussed at some length. After that, Ahmed decided on the menu. We settled down in our apartment, grateful for the peace and tranquility, letting the gentle lapping of the water lull us to sleep.

Ahmed and his mate were up early. The boy, slipping along the narrow ledge outside our bedroom window, starting his day's work by lighting the fire in the old-fashioned boiler which heated the water for our morning baths. We felt cherished and cosseted in our little palace on the lake. Our houseboat was called Karnai Palace.

We woke early and stepped out on the porch, looked around us and saw the mist rise, saw boats swiftly gliding silently along and watched women gathering lotus leaves. We strolled along the gangway to the landing stage. Boats arrived. The florist, with his boat a riot of colours, greeted us gravely and we could not resist buying something. We bought some packets of seeds. We looked around, letting our eyes travel along the wooded slopes of the hills and the high mountains beyond. The sun rose, kissing the tops of the mountains and greeted us with loving glory.

Another boat arrived. A dignified, elderly gentleman introduced himself as Mr. Taylor and promised us special 'morning price', if we placed our orders there and then. It was difficult to refuse any offer when everything around us spelled luxury. His young helper produced samples of soft gentle Kashmir wool and glorious rich wild silks. Before we had time for regrets, orders had been placed and measurements taken. Payment? This was a minor detail and would be settled later. At no time was settling bills a problem in Kashmir. Anything and everything was accepted.

We joined our fellow travellers for breakfast. There was Lorna, the woman who had been guarding the gear at London Airport. She was a retired headmistress who always knew better than everybody else. She had married late in life. Her husband Frank was a widower with a grown-up family. Had she not 'taken pity on him, he would have curled up and died', that is what she told us. The couple had continued to live in their respective homes, some forty miles apart. Lorna had severe bronchitis from the day we arrived until we left, but would not accept any help offered. She shared a room with Meggie, a pharmacist from Liverpool. She was a very nice lady with a keen sense of humour, but she had shocking teeth. The second couple in our houseboat were Paddy and young Jean. Paddy - this was not her real name but she was generally known as Paddy - was extremely good company. She worked for the B.B.C. and was an extrovert through and through. She was amusing and a good companion to climb mountains with. Young Jean was a strange creature. Where fact stopped and fiction began was difficult to decide. She told a cock and bull story about her past. She was in her late twenties. It was Buddhism which saved her. She used to spend weekends in a Buddhist Monastery in Scotland and had come on this trip bearing gifts and messages from the lamas to their brothers in Ladakh. Strangely enough, she never told me about her turbulent past. Poor Jean, she had saved from her meagre salary for the past five years to be able to come on this trip. She was obsessed by the idea that every male in the party was trying to make a pass at her.

The rest of our group lived on the Acropolis. Rebecca shared with Barbara, the journalist, our 'Venerable Member'. She was a delightful person, full of fun and sheer love for living. She was good to be with. The male members of our party were our leader who, frankly, lived with his head in the clouds. His name was Oleg. Henry, a very knowledgeable potter who was steeped in Buddhism was the second male member of our party. He was an eccentric moving in his own little world, but interesting to engage in conversation, provided one was able to keep him to one subject. He found it extremely difficult to make decisions, but some how managed to get his own way most of the time. Big John, a consultant physician, kept himself very aloof to begin with until he too became involved. The nicest man of them all was 'John the Bird'. He was a person without guile, open and sincere. He and Barbara could not think ill of anyone. He was a very keen and extremely knowledgeable bird watcher, a conservationist, a climber and naturalist. He was a first class photographer and lectured about his trips. He carried fascinating recording gear around, which enabled him to take slides and also record sound. He was at all times considerate, never inconveniencing the rest of our party - a thoroughly nice person. Later, before leaving Srinagar and Dal Lake, Shirley, an American journalist, and Mr. Singh, our guide from Madras, joined us. Strangely, only Ruth and myself had come as a twosome, all the remaining members of our group had come on their own. However, Rebecca knew our leader, who had taught her husband Botany. Henry also knew Oleg well. I do not know where these two first met. In spite of the different personalities it was a good party and somehow we all seemed to settle down quickly and easily into a 'family atmosphere', without any feeling of commitment for the future.

Our first day on the lake was a Sunday. We set off in three shikaras after breakfast. The boys, sitting in the stern of each boat, made a feeble attempt at holding the boats together with a piece of string, but of course we parted company from time to time. At least we'd started off as a cavalcade! We passed the other elaborate houseboats with their funny names, some of them promising 'latest sanitation', some owner-occupied others to let. After these boats came the simpler ones, which were obviously let rather than used as hotels like our two. These were still nicely kept, still with names of kings, queens, past glory. We entered different waters and here on simple, wooden barges, lived large families. The children were water-babies, fearlessly jumping from one boat to another, perching on rickety roofs to watch us go past. We could look into these poor homes, whose only belongings were bed-rolls and cooking pots. These were cleaned in the dirty waters and polished with sand until they shone like silver. The children, with their clean faces and lively large brown eyes, were in rags, the women coyly hiding behind shawls, also poorly dressed. We passed a dilapidated house, proudly proclaiming 'River Police' and entered the River Yhelum, which runs through the centre of Srinagar. This of course was the most interesting part of the trip, since both banks were lined by houses. These were mostly built of wood on brick foundations. The windows appeared to reach down to the floor and were always wide open. In fact I doubt whether they had panes at all. Every opening was crammed with inquisitive faces watching our progress. These houses were incredibly tall with many storeys. It was a most odd architecture, if you could call it such, somehow reminiscent of mid-European Medieval style. Each building with many wooden balconies and numerous additions haphazardly stuck on to the original design, threatening to collapse under the weight of their human burden. We caused great amusement and good-natured laughter as we passed by. Many families with numerous children were performing their ablutions in the muddy waters or were laundering their garments, such as they were. We saw a chicken fall into the water and swim until it was rescued and brought back on to terra firma once again. Carpets and curtains had been washed and festooned high bridges in order to dry in the hot sun. We glimpsed the golden roof of a Hindu shrine, shimmering in the bright light.

At one point our three boats came adrift struggling against the turbulent stream. One of them almost capsized. Because of these difficulties we made for the nearest landing stage and came ashore to stroll through the narrow lanes and marvel at the numerous stalls, offering all kinds of merchandise, fruit, food, spices, clothing, silverware. We saw tall Muslim women completely shrouded from head to foot in their garments. The cloth fell in many fine pleats from a small skull-cap down to the ground. A lacelike inset across their faces enabled them to breath and to see. The older women, or maybe the married ones, wore cream only. The others were clad in brown or black. We walked past a broken Seljuk temple, through dusty squares, where old-fashioned goods lay side by side with plastic articles. We were content to look, listen to the strange sounds, absorb the aroma of unknown spices and to feel the hot sun on our skins.

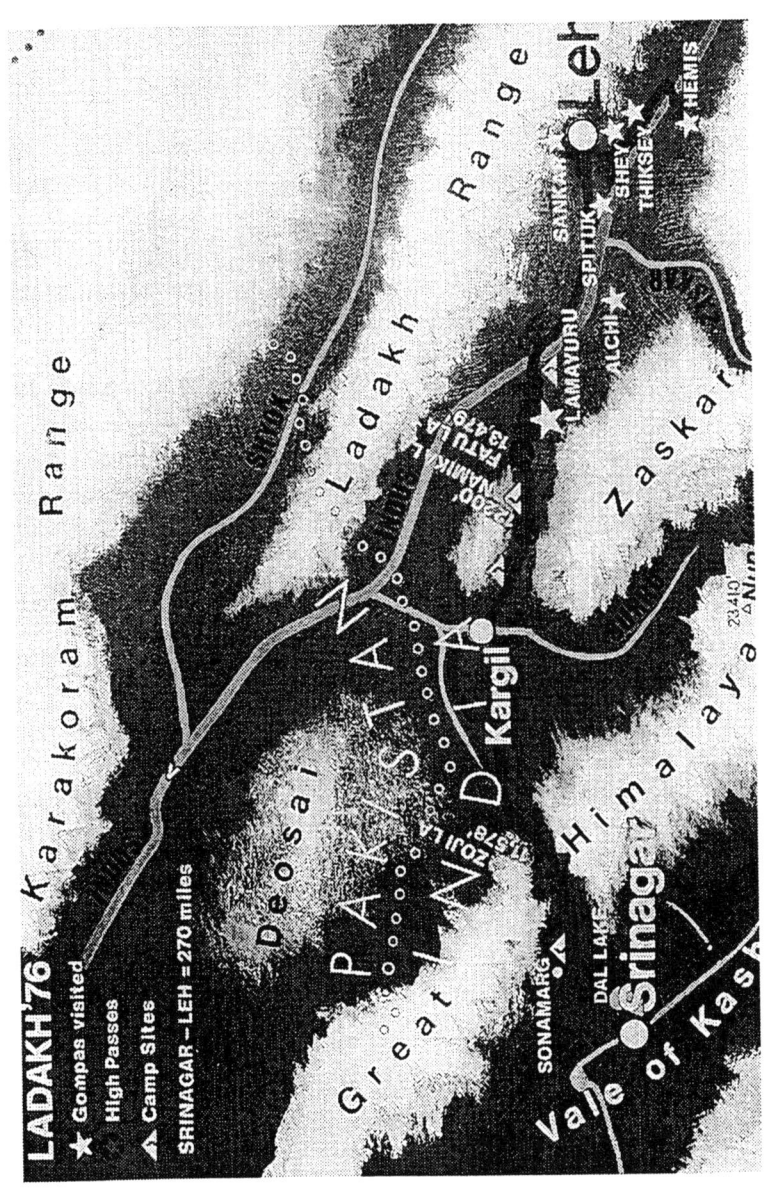

Map of Srinagar, Dal Lake and Ladakh.

'Home, sweet home'.

We walked past a mosque which looked like a pagoda and we looked down on a timberyard at the water's edge and at the corn market next to it. We stepped back into our boats again further upstream, and returned to our respective homes.

Back on our houseboat, stretching out luxuriously on our sun-drenched porch, we were visited in turn by various traders. Every article which was displayed for us to inspect was perfect in it's craftsmanship, and the expertise of the respective salesmen and of the one and only saleswoman was superb. The only lady was the 'Tibetan Woman'. She reigned supreme on the lake and was treated like an honoured guest when she came aboard. It was our first contact with a Tibetan. Her features reminded us of the Lapps in Scandinavia. She brought lovely Tibetan trinkets. We bought a little wooden bowl with silver filigree base, which is still much used and cherished by us. Then the young man with his embroidered Kashmir textiles arrived, comprising exquisite scarves, shawls, table-cloths, dressing gowns. One shawl was so delicate that it could be pulled through a wedding ring. Unfortunately one cannot buy everything one sees and we knew that there was more temptation to come.

We crossed the lake in the afternoon and drifted away in small groups. Paddy, John 'the Bird' and I joined forces and climbed the hill known as 'The Throne of Solomon', stopping from time to time to listen to a bird, look at a plant, admire the view down onto the lake, and glance across to the surrounding mountain ranges as we climbed higher and higher. The 'Char Chinar', the 'Island of Four Plane Trees' on the lake formed a distinct landmark seen from above. We reached the summit. Under the shade of an ancient tree an enterprising gentleman was selling tea brewed in a silver samovar. A small stone temple, a Hindu shrine, built in the eighth century, crowned the plateau. We took our shoes off and climbed up the steps to the sanctum which appeared strange to our European eyes, containing a bell and small figurettes of stone, half men, half beasts. We spent a long time admiring the majestic panorama in the fading light. The pink glow spreading over the highest peaks reminded us of the 'Alpine Glow', well known in the Dolomites as well as in the Alps. Angry clouds gathered above a far distant saddle of yet another mountain range. Filled with contentment, which only the sight of mountains can instil in me, we returned to our boat.

It was Ahmed who decided which trader was permitted to call on us and it was he who set the time. A young boy arrived with jewellery, beautiful precious and semi precious stones set skilfully in silver or gold. The leatherman followed, tempting us all with hats and coats, gloves and sandals, embroidered suede waistcoats and shirts. Again, no one could resist buying outright or placing an order.

Next morning all of us rose early, having appreciated Ahmed's early morning cup of tea. We set off in three shikaras once again, before six a.m. Mist was still lying low on the water, the sun was trying to rise, it was a magic hour of peace and silence on the lake. Swiftly and skilfully our boat glided through waterways with trees either side dipping their branches into the water, past man-made islands with market gardens, wells and large homesteads beneath the enormous trees. Life was beginning to stir. Families rose and stretched their limbs to greet the day, to wash in the still waters, to kindle fires. Birds flew across our path. We were delighted by the tameness of the kingfishers which abounded on the lake. We saw women collecting lotus leaves which provided the only source of fertiliser for the market gardens on the islands. We watched men with long poles skilfully scooping up mud from the bottom of shallow waters to use to build up other floating islands by placing this material between poles which had been securely fastened into the bed between the lotus plants.

Silence and peace were suddenly shattered. Boats laden with fruit or vegetables arrived from all sides, skimming the surface of the lake, skilfully manoeuvered by old and young alike. The sun had risen when we arrived at 'Convent Garden' on the waters of Dale Lake. The magic moment was destroyed by the incredible babble of voices of vendors and buyers conducting their daily business. Boats, full of well known fruit and vegetables, such as melons, cucumbers, aubergines, kohlrabi - in fact whole mountains of kohlrabi - were there, beside many unknown fruit and vegetables. In one part of the market was a 'Coffee Stall', which was of course a boat presided over by a buxom lady selling cakes and drinks. It was a colourful

'Shikara', watertaxi on Dal Lake.

'Quash' on the floating market.

scene which we were reluctant to leave. We were offered some pods of the lotus flowers by our little boatman as a parting gift, which we accepted gratefully. On our return journey we passed a floating 'village store', bearing all commodities on the slender craft.

Fortified by Ahmed's splendid breakfast, we set off to explore the town on foot. We walked through the bustling city to the boundaries in order to obtain a good view of Fort Man Parbai, which spanned the top of a hill. This had been built in the sixth century and looked quite splendid. Below the Fort stands a Hindu temple and at the foot of the hill lies an old Hindu graveyard, where cows grazed peacefully amongst the ancient gravestones. We turned towards the centre of town again, crossed a sunbaked square to visit the Friday Mosque. This was a wooden building, pagoda-like in architecture, centred around a peaceful, grassed courtyard. As if by special design, a mullah stood in the middle of the courtyard, surrounded by thousands of pigeons, many encircling his turbaned head. The Mosque itself was lofty, with tall, wooden pillars supporting the manifold roofs, like trees soaring up to heaven. We completed our tour with a visit to a carpet factory. This proved most interesting. The original factory had been started by the British. They had left the looms and all machinery behind, on the condition that it would be run as a co-operative enterprise. This had been adhered to. In fact it was run by families who carried on their tradition, which went back centuries. Highly skilled artists used ancient designs and wrote these down on graph paper rather like music, with special keys indicating various motifs. A code was used for the various colours. Each pattern was set down on a long strip of paper which were collected to form long books. One family worked on one loom. To our amazement we saw children aged from four to twelve, boys only, working on the looms. They were big-eyed children who wielded their combs and curved knives deftly. An adult called out the code for colour and design. The boys were delighted to see us and quickly moved aside to make room for us to squat down amongst them. They proffered their tools to us so we could have a go and were hugely amused at our clumsy efforts.

We were taken into the showroom. Most glorious carpets were

unrolled to be displayed in all their splendour for our benefit, although everybody was fully aware that none of our party were in a position to buy their exquisite carpets. We could sense the pride with which the salesman displayed his wares. It was a pleasure to watch him and share his admiration for the superb craftsmanship which we were privileged to sample. A special golden one caught our attention. The shades varied according to the pile. 'John the Bird' took a photograph of Ruth's carpet and later sent us a copy.

We set off once more in our water taxis after lunch to visit the famous Mogul gardens. This time we drove away from town along the lake. We had a Sikh driver and a very gentle, bearded Kashmiri guide. The first garden lay at the foot of beautiful rugged mountains, which formed a backcloth, whilst the lake made a splendid foreground. An arch lead on to the sun-drenched lawn. Numerous majestic Chinar (Plane Trees) were planted in this garden. The Chinar Tree was the pride and joy of Kashmir. Simple flowers of great variety grew in happiness and abundance side by side. Below a shady apple tree sat an enterprising little old man with a pair of scales, selling apples from the self-same tree. An Indian family, the ladies dressed in bright saries, played ball games with careful grace. The crystal clear waters from the mountains behind ran into a spring, which surfaced in a simple pavilion at the end of the garden. This garden was called 'Nasim Bagh', which meant 'Royal Spring'. By its position above the lake, nestling against the flank of the majestic mountain, the hot sun was always tempered by a gentle breeze. We lingered for some time at this peaceful spot before continuing along an excellent road to 'Nishat Bagh', which was world famous for its fountains and cascades. Sadly all water had been turned off, not a single fountain was playing, no pool reflected the sun. It looked neglected and derelict, with grass and weeds growing in the basins where lotus flowers used to grace the clear waters. It must have been a magnificent sight once upon a time, with ten terraces gently leading down towards the lake and what must have been a very graceful pavilion in the centre of the garden. It was still lovely, but bore an air of decay. We were compensated by watching the little Hooper bird at close quarters and by obtaining a photograph of it in the fading sunlight.

We visited the last garden, 'Shalimar Bagh', the 'Garden of Pleasure', built by Jahangir for his favourite wife. He used to spend the hot summer months here with her, his 'Light of the World'. Srinigar served as summer capital of the former Kashmir state. As we walked along the flagged path, stopping to watch the gardeners, the sun was slowly sinking into the lake. A man and a woman were trimming the grass verges with short, hooked knives. It looked so easy that we indicated that we would like to try our hand. But once again we proved to be clumsy, compared to the simple gardeners. We climbed up the many steps leading to a gazebo at the end of the garden. We watched a most picturesque sunset over the lake through the lacy veil of the branches. Well satisfied with yet another splendid day, we returned once again to Ahmed's warm welcome and to his solicitude for our comfort. Later that evening we called at the 'Acro Palace' for drinks, sharing the bottles which each of us had purchased at London Airport. It seemed almost a lifetime ago since we were waiting for our journey to commence.

The following day, having again crossed the lake in the now familiar transport, we set off for a day trip into the past up into the mountains. Again, three taxis stood waiting for us near the landing stage. We drove through the lovely valley of Kashmir, green and lush, fertile and well-cultivated, with orchards of peaches, apricots and almonds, with mulberry trees used for silk production, with green barley fields and yellow rice paddies. And everywhere the king of trees, the lovely Chinar Tree was in evidence.

We reached the first Hindu site. This was a temple dedicated to Siva. Little remained of the actual structure, but the ground was littered with fragments of stone sculptures, which never failed to thrill me.

The second Hindu temple was also built in the same era by the same king, King Avantivaman, who ruled from 855 - 883. This temple was dedicated to Vishnu. More had been preserved of this ancient building. We entered through a handsome gateway and noticed the splendid peristyle with some exquisite carvings on the columns, with the sacred goose well in evidence. We found it quite exciting to admire the many fragments of marvellous stone carvings and enjoyed taking photographs. Some of the lofty arches, supported by columns, were faintly reminiscent of Gothic architecture.

The last of the ancient Hindu excavations were the ruins of Martand. Beautifully situated on a plateau above the valley, this lofty building reminded us of Durham Cathedral. It had been built between 724 - 760, probably to worship the sun god. It was the biggest Hindu temple in Kashmir and had most graceful arches and soaring columns.

On all these sites the local population came out to see us and were most friendly, always eager to have their photographs taken and to hand us their addresses. We returned to England with a number of names and addresses and, in due course, the respective photographs were despatched to the appropriate corners of Kashmir.

We continued through dense woods, reaching a village which produced cricket bats. I do not know whether all cricket bats were manufactured here, but certainly the whole village appeared to be one enormous factory making cricket bats to despatch all over the globe. We passed small homesteads along small brooks where wool was being dyed and where a cottage industry of weaving and handicraft flourished. We arrived at the Hindu village of Antag. We admired the gaily decorated road carriers, which were the transport lorries of Kashmir and were most picturesque. For the first time we saw women in Kashmir dress, which looked like a nun's habit in pale blue. We entered the temple complex, and noticed some wild looking, swarthy hill people who sat on the ground looking slightly menacingly at us. They shied away from our cameras. Later we learnt that these were Gypsies. The complex consisted of a number of shrines, each presided over by its own guru. We were allowed to step inside one of them. At the centre of the temples lay a pool. Rather incongruously, a woman had come to this pool with her red plastic bucket. Apart from the shrines with their golden roofs serving as a place of worship, this was also a seat of learning and contained a large Hindu school. As everywhere in Kashmir, lessons were given under the open sky. We watched groups of small children at work. They were neatly dressed in dark blue uniform with Persil white shirts. They sat in a circle on the grass clutching their slates. They were taught in four languages, Hindi, Kashmiri, Urdu and English. The teacher called one little girl up and told her to step into the centre and demonstrate 'how we work and play'. It was quite sinister and frightening to see this little mite ordering her playmates about and really almost barking out commands, which were executed without any trace of resentment, and without the slightest hesitation.

We left the little colony and climbed higher into the mountains. The scenery resembled Switzerland with rocks, clear mountain streams, fir trees replacing their leafy comrades. The local colour remained, there were monkeys in the trees. We reached Phalgan, a famous summer resort. It had only one main road, which was flanked by shops. Some of these sold exquisite jewellery. The atmosphere was like a frontier town with wild horsemen riding in, tethering their steeds outside their lodgings. Past the main street lush meadows lay . Horsemen waited here with their ponies to be hired out for rides and for trekking. Newly built wooden chalets were dotted amongst the trees. We stopped by a clear mountain stream for our picnic lunch. Rugs were spread on the soft ground and each of us received a little plastic box with a lovingly prepared meal. Tea and coffee were served. It was the hour for mid-day prayer. Our kindly crew prostrated themselves without the slightest hesitation or embarrassment in order to praise Allah. It was Rhamadan and of course none of our Muslim crew would eat or drink between sunrise and sunset.

We went for a walk up the mountain side, past a village huddled below us, towards a golden field. Meggie was the only one amongst us who hired a pony, and rode past us up the steep track. We saw a wooden platform erected in the field. This served a man, poised with a gun, watching for prowling bears.

We stopped in the thick of a walnut wood on our return journey to buy some freshly harvested nuts. We halted as soon as the sun had sunk below the horizon for our driver to break his fast. It had been yet another splendid day, which even a slight shower of rain in the mountains could not spoil.

That evening we went to the Acro Palace to hear a young

Tibetan talk about Ladakh. He had fled his native Tibet when he was eleven years old. He had lived in Germany since then and had married a German girl. He worked at a university - the name of the town eludes me. He was doing research appertaining to Tibet. He had just returned from a six week tour to Ladakh with a German party.

Our last day on Dal Lake was a leisurely one. We all went to Srinagar for the most important transaction, namely to get to a bank and cash some travellers cheques. Confusion appeared to reign in the busy, completely open plan bank. Finally we were all in possession of adequate sums of Rupees. After this transaction, we each went our own way. Ruth returned to the boat, since she had felt slightly sea sick with the faint movement around our boat.

I joined Oleg, our leader, and Paddy. It was a good morning. We went through narrow lanes and watched craftsmen at their work. Only men worked in open-fronted shops. They designed most delicate patterns, they sewed, embroidered, did intricate basketwork, produced fine leatherwork and many more artistic articles. Oleg knew Srinigar well and led us to the proper market, where the local population bought their goods. We bought some most attractive cotton by the yard, admired the mouth-watering foodstalls and jostled with the crowds. Everywhere we detected typical Tibetan features. They were the traders, spreading their wares out on the pavement. I suddenly had to relieve myself and became quite desperate. Paddy came to my rescue and steered me unabashed into the narrow gangway of a house, proudly calling itself 'hotel'. All occupants appeared to be assembled in the kitchen, which was a dark 'Hole of Calcutta'. My dilemma caused no problems. I was led up a rickety stairway into a room with bare boards, an iron bed, a table and chair. A young man, obviously the inhabitant of this luxurious accommodation, was banished forthwith and I was allowed to use the hole in the ground in the adjacent closet in full privacy. Relieved in more senses than one, I was able to rejoin my partners to browse for some time in one of the government shops displaying a full range of Kashmiri goods. We stopped twice more, once in a shop where two Persian brothers sold their beautiful papier mache work and lastly in a bookshop.

Ruth was rested and fully recovered when I returned, ready for lunch. In the afternoon we crossed the lake. Whenever you were on the water, enjoying the perfect peace and apparent solitude, out of nowhere traders suddenly appeared offering almost everything from toothbrushes to furcoats.

We gently ambled up the 'Throne of Solomon', once again admiring the view, which was slightly marred by Mrs. Ghandi's slogans boldy displayed along the hillside. In the evening our last meal had been prepared in true splendour by Ahmed. He served us a Kashmiri meal. The table was beautifully decorated with garlands of flowers. The meal was concluded with fragrant Kashmiri tea, brewed in a silver samovar.

Our dream on Dal Lake had passed quickly. It was almost as if we had turned the pages in one of Somerset Maugham's well known stories. Paddy expressed our sincere thanks to Ahmed for his tender care in writing in the Book of Karnai Palace, and each of us at that moment hoped to return one day to recapture the immense pleasure and peace which we had experienced during our stay. I wonder if any of us will ever return?

'Stupa'

Ladakh

We packed up and bade farewell to Ahmed and our lovely houseboat on Dal Lake. We crossed the lake for the last time in the now familiar water taxi, enjoying the peace and beauty of it. Our bus was waiting for us at the landing stage, complete with two drivers, two cooks and two porters constituting our splendid crew. All were Muslims and most charming and solicitous in their attention to our needs. We took our kit bag containing two sleeping bags, two small pillows, nightclothes, tracksuits and one rucksack containing oddments. A cute jute zipbag held the remainder of our simple belongings, just a change of clothing and underwear. The remaining suitcase was left at the hotel in Srinagar, where we were booked for our return.

On the roof of our bus were live chickens for our meals. We collected firewood, vegetables and other food along our way. We skirted the lake, drove up through lovely forests and through golden fields beneath the shade of walnut trees until we reached a little town. This small community appeared to have the flavour of a frontier town. A medicine man sat on the ground mixing his potions, cattle were offered for sale, a little boy had been left in charge of a mountain of walnuts. The barber rushed out of his shop, which was a crude little shack, asking us to take his photograph. It really felt as though we had arrived in the Wild West.

We continued our journey and soon started to climb up a most fantastic pass. The roads were perilous, but fortunately our drivers were quite excellent. These highways were kept open by the army. They were entirely closed for three months of the year when the temperature dropped to around minus twenty degrees, and had to be blasted in the spring.

Our next stop was a big camp in the high valley of Sonamarg. A large number of ponies were milling around, ready to be hired for trekking. This was a favourite starting point for trekking, for walking up to high valleys, or to rest before climbing up to the lofty heights of the next pass.

It was crowded when we arrived with many tourists and crowds of poorly clad children and people in rags. The children were begging and watched us avidly while we had our lunch. We handed most of it to them, bread, chicken, fruit and biscuits. They were like little vultures. They were the poorest folk we ever met, appearing somewhat lost and misplaced in this majestic scenery. A strong wind blew cruelly at the foot of the high pass.

We drove up the beautiful, awe inspiring mountains to Dras. This is the second coldest place in the world, the coldest being Siberia. The army was very much in evidence. They provided the vital supply line and were always extremely helpful and friendly to us. Many of the drivers were Sikhs, who always had a cheery word for us.

A strange, brilliantly white building arose suddenly on the horizon. Our first 'Stupa'. These are holy shrines which originally housed the remains of saints, but were now used as burial mounds or simply as prayer shrines. We had to walk around all religious edifices in an anti-clockwise direction. Stupas, which were to become a familiar sight in the days to come, were difficult to describe without pictures. They were sometimes square, sometimes round, sometimes octagonal, frequently decorated with a relief of fictitious animals or plants. They were always crowned by a dome with a pointed spire soaring towards the sky. Sometimes they stood on their own; near homesteads we saw usually three stupas standing inside a gaily coloured small, open fronted shelter, or lined up in a row like soldiers on parade.

We passed a white house built into the grey rock, before we suddenly came face to face with an enormous statue of the Lord Buddha. The first impact was terrific. I cannot remember the dimensions, but it was quite gigantic, elaborately carved into the rock, towering high above the little wooden sanctum. Each sacred shrine, whether a statue or a building, was heralded by numerous 'prayer flags'. These were just scraps of material strung up on supple willow branches along the roadside or spanning across, fluttering in the breeze, inviting us to search for the holy place.

The nearby village of Mulbekh was our first Tibetan village, consisting of a small collection of large, square, brilliantly white buildings with gaily coloured wooden frames, painted in vivid red, blue and yellow. There were no windows inside these frames. The roofs were flat, so they could serve to store wood and dry fruit and vegetables for the winter. Occasionally an odd tent had been pitched up on the roof, a 'pent house' of Ladakh. Beneath the roof, faggots were arranged in a most elaborate fashion, end on and were also painted in the same vivid colours.

Having admired the gigantic Buddha of Mulbekh, we continued on our way. Rounding a dramatic bend, we blinked in amazement at the sight of our first Buddhist monastery. It lay before us like a picture in a fairy story. It was such a superb, dramatic setting that it almost looked like a stage set. The tall square buildings of Lamayuru Monastery crowned the tip of a spur of rock towering above the valley. Below the main buildings lay the courtyards and smaller shrines and houses for the monks. A small village huddled in its shadow. Further down, the valley was carpeted with soft, golden fields.

Most 'Gompas', Buddhist monasteries, lay in the most inaccessible locations, with steep paths leading to them. Utmost courtesy was the password when we arrived at the portal of any Gompa. Then our reception was assured and we were welcomed with dignified hospitality. The Lamas were sweet and gentle people with a ready, childlike smile, clad in dusty, dirty brown garb. Some of them sat patiently along the pathway, offering trinkets for sale. We were free to walk around the Gompas, climb up steep stairs, reach a flat roof from which we could gaze at the beautiful mountain ranges, and enter the dusty dark sanctum without shoes, so that we could peer at the magnificent wall paintings. We got to know the Buddhas - enormous ones, small ones, Buddhas with hundred arms, Buddhas with eleven heads, Buddhas with eight pairs of eyes. We learnt to recognise the mask of the evil spirits, we became familiar with the various symbols and admired the tankas, which were everywhere. These were silk scrolls exquisitely painted in exact, precise geometrical patterns with Buddhas and other deities. They were as esteemed by Buddhists as were the Icons by the adherents of Orthodox faith.

Life became more exciting, since every step led to a new discovery. We discovered the prayer-wheels, some elaborate, others quite simple, made from bone and silver or finely carved in wood or horn, others very simple, fashioned from old tins. These were essentially of the same principle as the Thora in our synagogues.

We sat within the view of Lamayuru, our first monastery, and were served with a lunch which had been beautifully prepared. We each received a little plastic box containing meat, egg, curry puffs, shredded salad, nuts, sweets, apples. Lemonade and tea to quench our thirst followed. All members of our crew were wonderful. Wherever we were at four pm., everything stopped for tea, 'English Tea', complete with cut cake was served.

It was a long, long day, this first exciting day of our journey to Ladakh. It was dark when we reached our first camp. Some German tourists had pitched their tents and kindly let us use their mess tent and even refreshed us with a welcome cup of tea whilst our crew erected our tents. Two hours later, having washed and changed, we were all once more assembled in the mess tent to partake of a three course meal, commencing with soup and concluding with tea. It was most remarkable the way in which food was presented; it would have done any first class western eating place proud.

We carried a strange contraption on the roof of our bus which heated water. It consisted of a special high wooden stool and two tanks. The cold water tank was placed on the stool with its tap directed into a funnel leading into the lower tank. The second tank stood on its own legs. This consisted of an outer jacket surrounding a central chamber, which served as furnace and was wood fired. The water was heated very quickly and could be drawn off from the tap at the bottom of the hot water tank. We learnt after our first night to get our bowl of hot water, to strip and wash, change into nightclothes and don our tracksuits before supper. Having eaten, we were ready to step into our sleeping bags in our little tent, just big enough for two. It was very cold at night. We, being new to camping, unfortunately had terylene sleeping bags, whilst the old hands were snug in their down sleeping bags. Barbara came to the rescue and lent us thick woollen socks. At least our toes were warm. No matter,

Lamayura village.

dawn and sunrise were magnificent and the true discomfort of the night was soon forgotten. It was great to be greeted by beautiful mountains and clear, bubbling brooks. We were called with a cup of tea before breakfast. Breakfast itself was an elaborate meal with cornflakes or porridge, fruit juice, eggs boiled or fried or as an omelette, bread, butter, marmalade and honey, tea or coffee to be chosen from. The mornings were crisp and clear and on our return journey, hoar frost covered the meadows as dawn broke, melting quickly away in the hot sun.

The journey continued amidst most extraordinary rock formations. Barbara, the journalist, and I used to let our imagination run absolute riot, seeing all sorts of things in these weird shapes. We passed through very few villages and shanty towns. Ladakh was still a kingdom and the princess was actually being married whilst we were there. Her husband was adopted into the Royal family, destined to become the future king. There was a younger son, but the lamas had not been able to pronounce him suitable to become king. By tradition in a Tibetan family, one of the sons, not necessarily the eldest, married and remained at home to continue the family and care for the older members. If there were only daughters, one married and her husband adopted the family and name and moved into the home of his wife to carry on the family. Tibetans were always known by their family name and by the name of their village. In former days brothers could share a wife. But this had been revoked by law about ten years ago. Basically Tibetan society was very simple. If fields were ready to harvest, the owner asked for willing hands to help. Everybody who had time to spare turned up to work, getting food and drink for the day. Next day it was somebody else's turn.

Our charming guide told us that his seventy four year-old grandfather still worked in the fields. They worked for nine months of the year, for the remaining three they were cut off from the world, with the temperature well below freezing point. Then they used the time to pray, to visit monasteries, to study. The gompas had big houses clustering around them, each monk occupying one house. His relatives came to visit and many stayed to study and sometimes decided to become lamas. Unmarried girls became nuns. Their hair was shaved, they wore the same habits as the lamas. Maybe it was a status symbol, more acceptable socially than being a spinster. They lived at home.

Each monastery had a large number of lamas, but few were in residence during the summer months. They were out working. A Buddhist monk was sent out with a begging bowl, since begging meant fulfilling a good deed by giving the donor a chance to do a good act. Life was simple and tranquil in the clean mountain air high up in the Himalayas. The climate was harsh. In summer the sun beat down relentlessly, in winter it was very cold.

We camped the second night along a tributary of the River Indus. We had descended from a pass down twenty-seven hairpin bends. The small camping place greeted us like an oasis, amongst young trees along the clear, green waters of the little stream. On the opposite bank stood a few humble dwellings, from which next morning some girls emerged to haul themselves along a rope across the ravine. They always carried a triangular wicker basket on their backs. Literally everything and anything went into this. They collected cow dung to dry for their fires, twigs for kindling wood, berries and other things nature provided. When we broke camp, everything - bottles, cans, food was swiftly scooped up into their baskets. Cans were used to protect the stems of young saplings from the ever-nibbling goats. Later in Leh, the capital of Ladakh, we found that they cleverly transformed them into mugs, funnels, lamps. By pressing out the cans into sheets, they could use them for almost anything, especially the big tins. We had seen this of course in Ethiopia, where nothing was wasted.

We had decided after breakfast to walk on, rather than wait for the bus to be ready to leave. Apart from breaking camp, packing and clearing up, there was a delay since a fire had to be lit underneath the bus to start the engine. We could not loose our way since there was only one road leading to Leh.

It was lovely, trotting off, lingering to savour a view, stopping to talk to any Ladakhian we met, taking photographs, catching up with a member of our party. I noticed that Shirley, the American journalist, who mostly worked producing photographs, was limping.

I did not want to ask why. I thought maybe she had twisted her ankle. We walked along the emerald river, cuttings its way through rock to join the Indus.

The bus caught us up and we all clambered aboard. We were anxious about Barbara, who was suffering from the altitude. She was 69 and suffered from high blood pressure and was rather large. She decided to come with us to walk to Alchie, one of the famous monasteries. One of the porters looked after Barbara, anticipating every necessary move. In fact we had three casualties on this outing. Young Jean from Newcastle had a bad cold and felt quite poorly when we reached Alchie. 'John the Bird', the nice man from Edinburgh, suffered from altitude sickness and was far from well. He did not join us on this outing, but remained on the bus.

It was a steep climb. Looking back, we saw our little stream and numerous groups of small stupas scattered around the ripening fields. We reached a high plateau. It was exceedingly pleasant to amble along, to admire the beautiful panorama, to watch the cattle, the yaks, cows, goats and sheep, to talk to people as they passed. There were children on their way to the monastery, walking for miles, bearing their gifts. There were women carrying bundles of hay, and men looking like tinkers with all their worldly goods on their backs. Everybody was delighted to stop and smile and was fascinated to look through our fieldglasses. We passed many 'mani', stone walls built with flat stones, which had most exquisite, delicate carvings on many of them. They appeared to be quite casually placed on a heap. I was not certain whether they were burial walls or wayside shrines. I rather think that each pilgrim as he passed on his way, added his stone to the wall in order to say that he too had been there.

As we drew nearer to the monastery, we heard singing. The farmers were threshing corn and chanting whilst they worked. We passed through an archway to enter the gompa. The portal had lovely paintings on its ceiling. We were, as always, most courteously received and taken round. Rooms were specially opened for us, their most cherished treasures, however dusty they were, proudly displayed. They did not mind if we wanted to take photographs and even flash lights were allowed.

We sat in the monastery gardens eating our lovingly prepared lunch out of our little plastic boxes. We had been greeted with refreshing lemonade when we arrived after our steep climb, feeling hot and covered in dust.

Coming along to Alchie, 'Big John', the consultant from the Lake District, had pointed out to me that Shirley had developed foot drop. I asked her at this point whether she had hurt her foot. She thought she had twisted her ankle. The going was rough and until we could find a stick for her, she held onto my shoulder, which was the right height for her to gain support. Then a lama presented her with his staff. Coming back I looked after Barbara, and Big John after Shirley, who had great difficulty in walking by then. This started quite a bit of a drama. Young Jean had been sent back to the bus with one of our porters.

We arrived in Leh, where we stayed in a guesthouse. We had a double room, which was just a square box with two iron bedsteads. We used our sleeping bags as before. There was an European toilet as well as the usual hole in the ground. One little boy, with a canister strapped to his back, spent all day going back and forth to the village well and climbing up on the flat roof on a rickety ladder to fill the tank for us to be able to flush the loo. The bedrooms surrounded the square hall, which was roofless and open to the sky. An open staircase led up to the first floor to our sitting room, which was covered with carpets, all other floors being plain stone without any rugs. There were chairs in the lounge, but we usually sat on cushions on the floor, beside low tables which had little bowls containing toasted barley flour placed upon them.

Our crew had pitched their tent in the forecourt, where they slept. They cooked all our meals in the yard at the back of the hotel, outside the dining room, which was a bare room with rough tables and benches situated in an outhouse. It was all very primitive, but nice and everybody was extremely friendly, welcoming us with open arms. The owner, a charming ex-army man from Madras, had married a Ladakhian girl and settled very happily in Leh. A most delightful Ladakhian girl, who we called Mathilda, served at table. Menus were seriously discussed and dished up most artistically, however

Shey Gompa.

Fields of Tikse Gompa.

Ladakhian farmer.

humble the ingredients.

I tucked young Jean into bed with hot drinks and aspirins when we arrived at the guesthouse. Poor youngster, she really did feel sorry for herself. We then had a look at Shirley. Pompous John decided that she had developed multiple sclerosis and that it was imperative for her to be treated with steroids. Leh is a garrison town with a military air strip and a military hospital. Mr. Singh was our Indian guide. He was a silly young man, who had lost the dignity of his native India without acquiring the knowledge of the West. He had lost his identity. But he was eager to please at all times, a very Indian trait. He tried to contact the army doctor and succeeded. The doctor insisted on coming and seeing for himself. A little man appeared the next day. He was visibly not impressed by the diagnosis, nor was I. The steroids that John wanted were only available in Bombay. He offered an alternative. We had to borrow the one and only syringe in the whole of Ladakh to give poor Shirley an injection, which in my opinion was an unnecessary exercise. I became very upset when I realised that John decided to tell Shirley, rather romantically on the flat roof under the starlit sky, that she had multiple sclerosis.

Next day we set off to visit the local monastery. Shirley remained near the bus. She was soon surrounded by children. She talked to them and used her lipstick and eye-shadow to make the little girls' faces up. We continued and visited another monastery, high on a hill, where John made Shirley climb up. It was a splendid complex. The courtyard was used for the ritual of the Dragon Dance. Our young Ladakhian leader explained the Wheel of Life to us in a most simple and touching way.

We drove through fertile valleys and heard the drumming and chanting of four musicians. They sat on the ground and played on a flute and three different drums. Boys and men of all ages squatted on the ground in one line holding a stout scythe in their right hand. Almost at the word 'go', they started in unison grasping a bundle of corn in their left hand, cutting with their right hand, and moved quickly and deftly forward in step. A second team followed, throwing ropes on the ground and collecting a bundle of the cut corn. Usually this was a woman, who then sat down in front of the bundle of cut corn, taking the four ends of the two ropes over her shoulder. The man, who had collected the bale, stepped in front and, grasping the ropes, literally hauled woman and corn up in one swift, coordinated movement. Securely on her feet with her load on her back, she would trot off chanting merrily. The whole process was fascinating and it was remarkable how quickly the field was cut.

We continued our journey along the dusty road through barren, stony valleys way beyond Leh. At one point our road was closed, the army was repairing it. This did not hinder us, we simply drove across the rough terrain until we could pick up the road again to travel up a narrow valley until we arrived at an oasis. We looked down on terraced fields. Here we stopped to take our splendid lunch near a little sparkling brook, before walking through golden woods to the most important monastery - that of Hemis. It was superbly peaceful with the sun streaming through the trees, forming patterns on the dry sand. The path wound upwards, following the clear stream. The imposing buildings of Hemis surrounded a large courtyard, which slumbered in the hot mid day sun. It looked very dilapidated, but one could easily bring it to life in one's imagination, transforming it into a crowded scene anxiously awaiting the start of the ritual dance around the majestic tanka, which was hoisted just once every ten years on its giant pole. We had hoped to meet the head lamas, but they were all away at Leh Palace for the wedding of the princess. We always managed to just miss them.

We had learned to recognise various statues, usually cast in bronze. We knew what to look for and began to become familiar with different signs and symbols. There were always little bells made of silver or silver alloys for offerings, small figures made from butter and sugar were always placed on tables. These seemed equivalent to lighting candles in the Catholic churches. We admired the elaborate silver jugs, the large attractive copper jugs, the beautiful candlesticks and fascinating horns, all these objects were for ceremonial use.

In one of the monasteries we were greeted with great solemnity and offered yak tea from a communal, fine china cup. This precious article, when not in use, was kept on a silver stand, and covered with a silver lid. Once we realised that indeed it was broth, not tea as we knew it, it became quite acceptable. It was made by boiling green tea with milk, seasoned butter was added. It had to be served very hot. I also had a morsel of sweetmeat offered me by a smiling lama, when I asked what the marzipan-like lump was. We always left some money and sundry gifts, such as pens, for the monastery, which appeared to make the lamas happy. They seemed child-like and took great delight in looking through our fieldglasses.

Here on Hemis Monastery, the largest in Ladakh, Shirley almost collapsed. This was not a physical collapse, but a mental and emotional state of exhaustion, since her leg was improving and in fact by the time we got back to Kashmir, there was no trace of disability left. I felt at the time that it had been quite unnecessary to tell her that she had disseminated sclerosis. It was a cruel thing to do, regardless of whether the diagnosis was correct or not. It was neither the time nor the place; nor had any of us the moral right to do so. None of us knew her, we knew nothing of her background, her personal relationships, her economic status. I think it was wicked and cruel, and yet I did not have the courage of my conviction to challenge big John. I had one opportunity, high up in the mountains, to speak to her on her own. After that, John monopolised her and she obviously took everything he said as gospel truth. I did tell her that I thought the diagnosis incorrect and would not accept it unless confirmed by expert neurological opinion. I thought that she had temporarily damaged a nerve, sitting in the lotus position after a long and tiring day. Unfortunately the damage had been done, the seed had been sown and the poor woman had been through hell and through mental agony and extreme anguish whilst in a strange country, surrounded by strangers. We did receive a letter from her, talking about our journey, talking about the weather and thanking me for my kindness. I still do not know more about her.

Back to the monasteries again. In one of them, Spituk Gompa, we were asked to watch a prayer session, which was known as Puja. We all sat on the floor, facing the lamas, who sat in a row with lighted candles and their traditional silver jugs and other vessels. They had drums and flutes and soon they began drumming and chanting. We were able to take photographs and 'John the Bird' actually taped the service. They did not mind at all. It was most exciting.

We were still pottering around up on the flat roofs admiring the views, when our Ladakhian guide translated the lama's question: 'Is there a doctor in the party?' Since big John was too busy taking photographs, I stepped forward. A poor lama appeared, supported by his brothers. He was moaning and groaning. He had a badly infected wound on his leg. I explained that I would be happy to help, but had nothing on me. We arranged for one of the young lamas to travel back with us to Leh. I first gave him a bar of soap. Efficiently, we had been issued with a torch, carbolic soap and a towel when we first pitched tents. The soap found great use. I instructed the young lama to begin treatment by washing his own rather grimy hands, before tackling the patient's leg. To do this three times a day. I handed him antibiotics and gave concise instructions on their use. He was obviously happy and promised a special Puja for Shirley. He had tea with us, before setting off merrily on his way to walk twelve kilometres back to Spituk Gompa. People here walked for miles to reach their monasteries. We often saw children with a goat or other life-stock on their long trail to a monastery.

We went to an open air 'Cultural Show' on our last evening in Leh. We sat on the ground amongst the local population. Men, women and children applauded the singing, dancing and the extremely expressive acting. It was great fun, but unfortunately it grew very chilly and we left before the end, which was a grand finale.

Young Jean had become very friendly with Matilda and admired her hairstyle, which consisted of two plaits interwoven with coloured braid. Jean had bought some of this special braid on our way up to Leh. Matilda joined us in the sitting room at night and plaited young Jean's hair into two, which she skilfully twisted around the crown of Jean's head. This labour of love completed, she presented her with a ring as a token of friendship. Matilda was a sweet and gentle person and everything she did was pleasing and suffused with gentleness. We in return gave her a little hairbrush as a parting gift.

India is basically a 'dry' country and in many provinces you cannot get any alcohol at all. On Indian planes or airports, if it is available at all, the price is astronomical. Most members of our party had bought some spirits at London Airport. I must admit it was agreeable to have a drink, particularly when camping. We even learnt to drink rum, even if it was pretty rough stuff. We had army issue supplied by our Indian Travel Agency. Our unfortunate Indian guide had the lion's share each night and subsequently never surfaced until mid day, when he emerged with a wet towel round his head. I used to tip mine into black coffee, which was not too bad.

On our last morning some of our party climbed up the hill which towered above Leh to see the view and a small monastery. Unfortunately Leh Palace, poised on this promontory, was locked. The view was superb over the higgledy, piggledy buildings of Leh to the military encampment across to the beautiful, all-encircling Himalayan Mountain. We found an artist at work restoring the murals in the small monastery, and had a long chat with him, arranging to call at his studio before leaving Leh.

Only a few from our party went along to his little house. It was just a concrete, square cube, containing three rooms. It was not finished as yet. He received us kindly. We all squatted on the floor whilst he showed us his sketches. He demonstrated the way he decorated dragons. He actually used an icing bag to make the 'blobs' of varying size. We were offered the customary tea. Before we parted, we bought two pencil sketches, one of a child's head, the other of a man in typical Ladakhian dress with a Tibetan dog by his side.

Some women wore hats which extended down their backs as far as their waists. These were studded with semi precious stones and formed their dowry. The men wore tall hats, reminiscent of Welsh hats.

I had often spoken to our gentle Ladakhian guide and since he suffered from a constant cough, I offered to give him some medication. One evening when he joined us he looked extremely worried. On questioning, he said that his mother had been taken ill. He asked me next morning, after we had left the painter, whether I would see her. She was a sweet lady lying on some bedding on the stone floor. She obviously had a temperature. Her chest was clear, abdomen soft. As

Our Host's wife in Leh

far as I could judge she suffered from gastritis. I left her some medication which I had on hand. The young daughter brought the customary tea and we parted best of friends. I asked our guide to let me know how the old lama, his mother and he himself were progressing, but sadly I never heard from him.

We had a great time walking up and down the only street in Leh, which was lined with shops as well as vendors squatting on the ground selling their wares. It was quite fascinating. We watched women teasing wool, men trading goats, selling fruit, offering trinkets of all kinds. We were pleased with our purchases, some prints of tankas to take home as presents.

We had promised to call on the wife of our host and managed to negotiate the rickety stairs to reach the flat roof, where we found her in all her finery. Shirley and big John had beaten us to it and were taking photographs. She was quite lovely and obviously delighted that we had called to pay our respects and was pleased for us to take her photograph. We left this happy place reluctantly.

We had talked to some French people and to an American couple who originally came from Germany, and a young Australian television producer. He had already made one documentary film about the Himalayas, which proved very successful when shown the previous year on television. This time he was gathering material to make a film about Tibetan refugees. We wished him luck.

'Progress' was being made. The Indian Tourist Office were building one hotel, whilst the Tibetan refugees were building another one in their own style. No doubt in the near future the military airstrip will be used to fly up from Srinagar in no time. I was so glad that we went then and saw Ladakh entirely unspoilt. We saw just one or two European 'drop outs', but not many. The climate was too harsh up in the high Himalayas. We met some enterprising young people who were travelling overland.

We left after lunch, amidst great farewells. Addresses were exchanged, photographs taken. Our drive back was quite breathtakingly beautiful. More impressive even than our journey coming to Ladakh. Whenever and wherever we stopped children materialised out of nowhere. We always handed out biscuits, dates or sweets. Once I received a newly-laid egg as a gift, handed to me with perfect grace by a solemn looking little boy. We drove over three high mountain passes. It was dark when we pitched our tents. It was also extremely cold and unfortunately we were short of wood, and the gas ring had broken. For once we had no hot water to wash in, no hot porridge next morning. But none of this stopped us enjoying the pure beauty of our surroundings. It was simply marvellous.

We walked a long way along the road next morning, enjoying the magnificent scenery. I had a small trowel to collect plants. We stopped at Kargil, a shanty town, to have our gas ring repaired. This was a Muslim village. Most of the able bodied men of the village watched the slow process of the repair of the gas ring. The women, however, were officially not in evidence, but we could see them in their colourful saris on the flat roofs. This town was no longer in Ladakh. No one knew the exact frontier. The other frontier, between China and Pakistan, was still in dispute. We left Kargil on foot before our bus was leaving. We walked slowly and leisurely amidst magnificent scenery, once again at peace with the world. Finally our coach caught us up and picked us up, one by one, until our party was once again complete.

The last pass which we negotiated was incredibly steep and narrow. Everybody held their breath until we reached the valley. We had arrived at Sonamarg, which meant Golden meadow, where we had had our first meal, which seemed an eternity ago.

Ponies were grazing, poorly-looking people living in tattered tents near the river minded the horses. That night our cook, half-blind though he was, produced a dish of diced meat garlanded by a ring of mashed potatoes and decorated with hard boiled eggs and tomatoes, followed by a cake topped with glace cherries and accompanied by real yellow custard. As always piping hot soup was the first course. Our crew were wonderful people.

Thick frost lay over the meadows when I stepped out of our tent next morning. I warmed my hands on the crew's little stoves. These were small clay pots - like our flower pots - set in baskets, which had two handles. Charcoal was lit to smoulder away. The pot was carried around beneath the torn, shabby Kashmiri blanket which everyone wore. Up in the rest-house in Leh, I always started my day with a cup of tea from the cook-house, where our crew began their work preparing breakfast. I watched them getting ready. They used a small twig to clean their teeth. They were such friendly people and obviously worked happily as a team. Mountains always create an atmosphere of special comradeship, and this certainly happened to our small party. At one point we even organised a laundry session, complete with line. The men got their Long Johns washed.

We stood outside the mess tent on our last morning, letting the sun warm our cold bodies, whilst we ate delicious French toast. It tasted great. We set off after breakfast, to do whatever we wanted. Big John, Paddy and I walked up the valley to the Hanging Glacier. Ruth went at her own pace, almost as far as we did. It was delightful to walk with ease uphill on springy turf, to amble through shady woods, to follow the path leading upwards alongside a bubbling brook. I collected plants all along the way. Big John, with long strides, was well ahead of us. Paddy was a comfortable companion. We talked when we wished to, we walked in silence, when this pleased us. We strolled ahead, each of us in turn, only to wait for each other further along to walk side by side for a little while. We caught up with Big John, sitting outside a shepherd's tent. We were offered tea by his wife, and John took photographs of the little family - the parents and their little boy. The woman asked for money, although the husband refused to accept; but we found an amiable solution, we slipped some coins into the child's hand.

We continued on our path through magnificent scenery. It had the same grandeur which I loved in the Alps and Dolomites. I collected many simple plants which I found exciting in this setting. On our way back, John rushed past us to meet up with Shirley, who had come up the valley on a pony. He handed her his gear to take it back for him and then hurried back to camp. Paddy and I lingered, watching some lovely shy birds. We saw a kid, just newly born. We savoured every minute of our walk. We met a party of Indians from the Punjab. The ladies were dressed in silken saris and high-heeled slippers, the men wore pullovers. I do not think that they ventured far up the valley.

We had spoken to some well-educated Indians before our trip. All of them pleasant, friendly people. I do not think that any of them saw the poverty and dirt which we noticed so acutely everywhere. I suppose if you grow up in this society you become conditioned, and dirt and poverty become an integral part of the general scene, melting into the background.

As we were nearing camp, one of the little scavengers begged for money. We had nothing with us. In a fit of temper, she peppered us with dung. How incredibly rich we must have appeared in the girl's eyes.

We reached camp in time for a 'Banquet on the Meadows'. A true Kashmiri meal had been prepared. This consisted of a hot rice dish, followed by delicious apricots. Young Jean had received fruit and barley wine from the lamas, to whom she had brought gifts from their brothers in Scotland. Hlava followed - this was less sweet than the usual Mediterranean version. The grand finale was Kashmiri tea, before we started on our last journey down to Srinagar. This was along a very dusty road. We stopped in a park at the shores of the lake. Tea was prepared for us for the last time, speeches were made and money was handed to our trusty crew. It was very moving, since everyone was most sincere, and found it difficult to put our heartfelt thanks into words. We spent our last two days in town staying at a modern hotel with a swimming pool. Pity that we did not return to our dreamy houseboat on Dal Lake.

We all dived into the bathtub, washed our hair, laundered our smalls and relaxed. Mr 'Taylor' arrived next day with our finished garments. He gently asked me for my rechargeable torch and for my silver pocket knife. I equally gently refused to part with either of them. I think that he did obtain some articles from his other customers.

We two strolled around town on our own. We looked and found the 'Park of the former Residence'. The Residence was being used as an Emporium of Arts and Crafts. I also found my way back into the Old Town and to the 'proper market', where the local population bought and bartered. We found the shop where we could purchase cotton dress lengths to bring back home. Finally I showed Ruth the lovely shop where they made and painted the charming *papier maché* articles. The old man sat asleep in the mid-day sun outside his store, looking for all the world just like another poor old man. As soon as we entered Aladdin's Cave, he was fully alert, quoting poetry at us: Omar Khayyam, Milton, Wordsworth, Shakespeare. His young son was sent forth to get tea for us, this time Kashmiri, not the Ladakhian variety. His younger brother joined the conversation. We bought some charming 'eggs' to give away as presents, and a lovely plate to add to our collection. The brothers were of Persian stock, their blue eyes denoting their origin.

We hired a three-wheeler taxi in the late afternoon to take us down to the lake to say goodbye - to Dal Lake, to Srinagar, to Kashmir. We drifted for the last time on the water as the sun sank slowly behind the magnificent mountains and dusk descended. As always, traders materialised out of nowhere and in spite of a firm 'no', we did succumb and bought a silver bangle, which was attractive and reasonably priced.

We spent our last morning around the pool at the hotel before driving to the airport, where pandemonium reigned. We had had problems in closing our suitcase, and had had to sit on it to get it shut. We had barely managed to secure our kit-bags, with all the purchases we had made. We had to open the kit-bag for inspection. I was worried, that if we had to open our case, I would be unable to close it again. I firmly stated that we had packed the case ourselves and it only contained our personal belongings. I kept repeating this statement over and over again to the smiling lady customs officer. She continued to smile and asked for cigarettes, which we did not possess since neither of us smoked. She asked for chewing gum; two pieces were all we had, and we handed them to the smiling lady. Our suitcase remained unopened. There followed the usual frisking. I had to hand over my pen knife. Needless to say, we were late taking off. Apparently no plane in India ever leaves on time.

Dusk was gently falling when we arrived in Delhi. Our Indian guide, who had left us once we had reached Srinagar, met us again with a bus at Delhi Airport. He had sent a very pathetic note to us all, addressing us as 'Dear Friends' and humbly apologising for his shortcomings. He did his best to show us the truly magnificent approach into New Delhi, which looked most impressive at night. We drove to an elegant hotel. After a good deal of confusion, since no one seemed to know the correct time of our departure, or whether we were meant to have a meal or not, we finally withdrew into our 'ladies department'. This consisted of a sitting room with a balcony, and a bedroom with a bathroom en suite. The men disappeared into their quarters. Beer was ordered. The time of our departure was still shrouded in mystery, and conflicting reports continued.

Jean disappeared with our Indian guide, Rebecca joined Oleg, Shirley had gone off with Big John. We had left Barbara behind in Srinagar to continue her travels in India. Everything appeared to be a trifle chaotic. We had a very hurried meal, but were unable to do it justice, which was a pity since this, our last meal, was the best we had had.

Ruth was worried lest Jean missed the plane. But true to form, the plane was late and Jean arrived in time. We all met up once more in the airport lounge. Finally we were off, but had to change planes in Bombay. A big Jumbo jet was waiting for us. In the frantic rush to catch the plane, our luggage was left behind. We had the usual comfortable flight, being fed at all hours, day and night. We read, we dozed, we talked. We touched down in Kuwait. We changed our watches.

It was daylight when we landed at Orley Airport, Paris. We were able to leave the plane. It was a nice airport, clean with a revolving gangway. It had been raining. Back on board again, it was only a short flight to London. Here we discovered that most of our luggage had been left behind at Bombay. This meant hanging about, filling in forms. But two hours later we were on our road back to our home; two tired, confused, but happy travellers. This was a marvellous trip which we shall not forget in a hurry.

P.S. We all met up once at the Overseas Club to see the excellent slides of John the Bird, accompanied by sounds, which he had skilfully recorded. Paddy and John the Bird came back to have a meal with us. That was the last time we had contact with these two. Henry, the potter, took us and Barbara out for a meal to the Indian Club in the

Strand. A funny place with oilcloth on the tables. Many years later we read of Henry's death. We ran into Oleg some years later at a lecture by Lady Betjamin about the Kulu Valley. I have his lovely book on the flora of the Himalayan Mountains. He died quite suddenly, aged 72. We lost touch with Barbara for some time, but met her quite by accident in the Strand. Since then we have become good friends. Fifteen years later, at the age of 84, this intrepid traveller went by train on her own to Budapest, Moscow, Ula Batur, Peking and finally to Hong Kong. Shirley, apart from the letter which I mentioned before, sent us some seeds from Australia. This was the last contact we had. We read a short time after our memorable trip that Big John led a party for one of the travel companies. Years later friends of ours met him and a new wife, a buxom, laughing lady called Bridget, on a journey in Peru. When we had returned from Kashmir and Ladakh, his very smart wife Theresa had met him at the airport. This is all the gossip I know which is linked to our wonderful journey.

Mexico
9 February 1978

It was 7 pm and night had fallen upon Mexico City at the close of our first day there. The traffic still remained as dense as it was the morning when I first looked down on the orderly four lane stream. The newspaper boys, dodging the traffic between the waiting cars, made brisk business when the traffic lights turned red. Reminiscent of Tehran, where we first saw this done.

It was good to start the day with a pink sky greeting us, before haze settled over the city. We had arrived after a long and tedious flight soon after 9 pm local time, the night before. This corresponded to 3 am, our time.

We had deposited our luggage at the air terminal on the eve of our departure and had continued to Knightsbridge to spend our last night with our Spanish friend, who has a brother in Mexico and asked us to post a parcel to him.

It was a bitter cold morning when we left London. The flight was long and boring, flying above the clouds in brilliant sunshine most of the time. It was by no means a smooth flight - we ran into strong gales after Bermuda. We were rather taken aback, since this sophisticated island had a very dilapidated-looking airport, which was very empty when we were there in transit.

Wind and rain greeted us. We continued our flight with a new crew on board. The staff were cheerful and served us well all along the way. The food was excellent.

We landed at Freeport after two-and-a-half hours' flight. It was a very stormy passage. At one time, we were literally thrown out of our seats up into the air. Freeport gave the impression of being a busy, elegant town. The scenery was flat with strange tall trees towering into the sky. Our last lap took just over three hours. The grand total of our flight was fifteen hours.

As good fortune would have it, a good friend recently returned from Mexico and gave me a book: Incidents of Travel in Yukatan by John L. Stephens. This is a delightful and fascinating book about an archeological expedition to Yukatan in 1841. I started to read as soon as we had settled in our seats and found it hard to put down. It certainly helped to pass the time. I had tried to read about Mexico before we left, since I knew nothing about this country. One book I read was a very factual account called The Mexicans - How They Live, packed with useful information. The second book The Lawless Road by Graham Greene I thought very biased, in spite of the fact that he is an excellent writer. It was the result of a special mission he went on in 1938 to ascertain the state of the Roman Catholic Church after years of horrible persecution. John L. Stephen's delightful account somehow helped to dispel Graham Greene's intense gloom. In fact, having arrived in Mexico and having left my daily cares behind, I was dipping into all sorts of books.

Let me continue with my first impressions before the second day dawns, endeavouring to put down my thoughts and comments from day to day as we travel along, hoping they will still add up to a coherent account.

We were greeted by a pleasant local guide on our arrival in the busy airport in Mexico City. A rickety old bus took us swiftly to the centre of town. It was Ash Wednesday and many of the brown-faced Mexicans had ashen crosses painted on their foreheads.

We are twelve members in our party. I shall reserve my comments for later, since we have not really had an opportunity to meet. They do not look an inspiring crowd. Perhaps this is hardly fair comment at this stage.

Already, from the air, Mexico City looked vast with a myriad of lights twinkling below the velvet sky. Betty, our travel companion, whom we had met in Ethiopia, remarked, "One city looks just like another when you first arrive." It was dark when we drove into town and we were very tired. We were thankful to get to bed. It turned cold that first night and we slept fitfully. We were grateful that we had organised our 'element' and could brew a welcome cup of tea at an unearthly hour of the night.

Traffic did not stop all night, but ran smoothly and continuously and did not disturb us unduly. Brash neon lights shone into our room. Dawn seemed to take a long time to come. Day did not start until seven o'clock.

We took breakfast in true Mexican style. A crude mug of steaming coffee, luscious tropical fruit - reminiscent of the Far East - toast and cakes. I had eaten cakes for breakfast in Spain before. Thus fortified, we set out on our explorations. Our first impression was that Mexico City is a lovely town. It struck us as surprisingly clean and quiet in spite of the volume of traffic and the numbers of cars parked cheek by jowl. There was no hooting, no shouting, and it was quite easy to negotiate the crossing of streets.

Now and again, policemen would stop us to ask if they could help us. They inevitably suggested a visit to the market and offered to get us a taxi. We declined these kind overtures. We strolled along the Paseo de la Reforma, which is a lovely broad avenue interspersed by open spaces, which have various monuments in their centres, or just beautifully laid out gardens. On both sides of the avenue are most delightful sculptures, some statues, others Grecian-like urns. The entire thoroughfare is lined with trees. The upper part of the Paseo is divided into a dual carriageway by gardens in the centre. These are most attractive and well cared for. Little dark-skinned old men with enormous Panama hats busily tend these gardens. Attractive stone benches are set amidst the greenery.

We walked in the warm sunshine, looking for a bank. No problem at all, since there is an abundance of banks in the Paseo de la Reforma. Either side is flanked by tall modern buildings. Most of these are hotels, banks, offices and delegations. In between these tall buildings stand delightful, small mid-European type private houses. This surprising aspect added to the pleasure of our morning stroll. We remarked on the high pavements, which would prevent the use of perambulators. However, all babies we saw were carried slung either over their mother's back or peeping out from under the colourful Sarapes, woven wool blankets with holes for the head, rather like the Kashmiri blankets we had seen the local population wear in Srinagar.

We passed interesting faces. It is a man's city with few women abroad, except poor Indians. Many of these squat on the ground with their little children clothed in rags by their side, offering nuts or sweetmeats for sale. Shops and offices started late. There appeared no shortage of eating places along the street. 'Shoeshine boys' were very much in evidence, but their boxes were not as elaborate as in Turkey. Nevertheless, business was very brisk. Their customers were always men - a woman never took the raised seat.

The Paseo de la Reforma is an elegant street. We enjoyed the glimpses into charming little sidestreets called Callas, which run off this splendid avenue. Some of these are pedestrian precincts, with pleasant trees in tubs and most delightful street lamps. We entered a church, rather new looking and simple, with a campanile of nine bells and a surprisingly austere interior. As always in Catholic churches, worshippers from every walk of life were earnestly engaged in prayer, oblivious to their surroundings. Happy and contented we returned to our hotel for a picnic lunch in brilliant sunshine on Betty's balcony. The morning had been a pleasant introduction to Mexico City.

After a short Siesta, we started out once more, strolling along the Paseo de la Reforma in the opposite direction from our morning walk. We found no difficulties in getting our bearings. The Paseo runs from North to West through the city and is intersected by callas at right angles. We noticed that the names of the callas to the right of the Paseo bear names of towns, such as Florence, Geneva, etc., whilst important rivers such as Rhine, Danube, Tiber, etc., gave their names to the callas on the left. Later we found another part of the city, where all streets were named after South American states.

It was a very hot afternoon. The mist had lifted and the sky was brilliantly blue, throwing the clear lines of the surrounding mountains into sharp relief. So far I have not glimpsed the 'Giants' of Mexico, Popocatepetel (the Snowy Mountain) and Iztaccithuatl (the white Lady).

We found Alameda Park just behind our hotel. This is a lovely park with Eucalyptus trees, date palms, sweet-smelling stocks side by side with brilliant irises and many other flowers. It was the peoples' park, with young lovers oblivious to the world around them, whilst the old dozed in the sunshine. Men, their eyes shaded by broad-brimmed straw hats, read their papers. Indians sat on the ground offering their tempting fruit. They deftly pick up a mango, impaled it on a stick, peeled it swiftly, cut it to resemble a flower, sprinkled it with sugar, dusted it with pink chilli pepper and handed it to their customer. Luscious pineapples, quite enormous in size, were neatly peeled and sliced and proffered on green leaves. Cucumbers were stripped of their skin and attractively disected to resemble an exotic plant. Oranges were prepared to look like lotus blossoms. As Betty remarked, the simple people we encountered introduced an almost oriental feature to the scene before us. Earnest-looking small children were playing near their mothers, making mud pies, as all children will do the world over, given the opportunity.

We left the park and passed the most imposing building, namely the Palacio de Belle Artes, with its impressive yellow dome. We were on our way to the one and only post office in Mexico City, a most remarkable building, one of the largest post offices in the world, with a very ornate facade. Inside it consists of a tall and lofty marble hall with enormous gold and black grilles between the customers and the ministering ladies. A long queue had formed at one position. All others looked very firmly closed, fastened with heavy chains. However, there was 'movement' behind the golden cage, and I planted myself firmly in front of the grille. Hey presto, a queue collected behind me. Carefully and pedantically the lady behind the counter organised herself. She placed a coarse, white cloth on the counter, displayed enormous stamps on either side of it. This done to her satisfaction, she counted all her other stamps. Our small parcel was finally weighed and stamped. But she indicated that it had not been fastened securely enough. We tried to get some of the gummed paper, which surrounded the sheet of stamps, from her. But she waved us to the back of the hall. Here, around a table, were people licking stamps and putting the precious surplus of serrated gummed strips carefully on the table for further use by people like myself.

This interesting mission completed, we emerged into brilliant sunshine to look for a market. Markets are features of Mexican life and every quarter of the city has one of its own. We now reached the poorer, older quarter. People were happily justling along through the ordinary shops with cheaper ware. We saw a lovely house, completely covered by blue Pueblo tiles. This had been a family mansion and now houses offices and shops. Opposite stood two very old churches. The Franciscan church was the first built by twelve Franciscan monks. Originally it had comprised a whole complex, consisting of a monastery and church with the usual offices, but only the church with its baroque facade and numerous chapels remains. The interior, in true baroque style, is very ornate with heavy gold-covered sculptures. We slipped into the second church, the Church of San Fillipo, named after a monk who died a martyr in Japan and was subsequently canonised.

It is difficult not to be carried away and mention these seemingly irrelevant tit-bits of information. But if one strolls through a strange city, with one's favourite guidebook tucked under one's arm, these little stories of no special consequence help to imprint this particular church, that particular statue upon one's mind.

We found the market, which reminded us vaguely of Hong Kong. Many little shops were housed within a pleasant, modern building. Needless to say, we could not resist temptation and made some purchases. We bought a very nice painting and some attractive glass boxes, assembled daintily with brass into unusual shapes. We also obtained a little pottery pig for a friend who collects 'pigs'. Later, in the museum, we realised that these pigs are of some significance. They were in evidence in plain pottery, dating back to antiquity. No one, however, could tell me why they were displayed in the museum.

Returning to the market: after a time one gets bemused, seeing such an abundance of the self-same article again and again in shop after shop. We had already stopped at the corner of the street to try on a chunky cardigan. We had resisted the temptation in spite of the fact that the asking price had been rapidly dropped by almost half.

On our way back to the hotel, we were attracted by a heavily ornamented, open door. The little porch which we entered contained the mechanism of a clock in a glass case. We walked further on into the church (the name of which I do not know) and were stunned by the brilliance of all the gold that met our astonished eyes. The gold of the altar decorations, in particular, was simply dazzling, whilst the display of plastic flowers, covered by plastic bags, was hideous, to say the least. The offerings in gold and silver to each specific saint seemed most touching. There is something very moving and child-like in this kind of worship. I can accept all the grandiose decoration and exuberance in these churches, since I feel that this lavishness is somehow of deep significance. I can understand how easily the Indians could assimilate this elaborate religion after their own colourful, ritualistic cult.

Tired but content, we returned via the pretty Alameda Park to our hotel for a bath and change before dinner, which we enjoyed at leisure before retiring to bed.

We woke early. Somehow we needed little sleep and found no problem with the altitude. The air appeared fresh and clear, reminding me of the atmosphere in Axum. We set off on our official city tour. It was nice to be already familiar with some of the landmarks in town. We drove along the Paseo de la Reforma, past the Palacio de Bella Artes, which has sunk below street level, past The House of Tiles and the two old churches. Nearby stands the Palacio de Iturbide, the most important building of the colonial period, in true Spanish style. It was the residence of the first Emperor of Mexico, and is now occupied by offices and shops. We reached the Zocalo, also known as Plaza de la Constitution. Every Mexican town has a Zocalo, equivalent to the Registan in Central Asia or the Agora of ancient Greece. This one is the second largest square in the world, the largest being Moscow's Red Square.

We admired the impressive facade of the Palacio National, built of grey and pink stone. Originally the Palace of Cortes, it now houses various government offices and the office of the President of Mexico.

The Mexican Independence Bell hangs above the central balcony. This is rung at 11 pm on the night of 15th September by the President, in commemoration of the liberation of Mexico, after his declamation to thousands crowding the Zocalo of, 'Viva Mexico! - Viva Indepence! - Viva Liberte!'

We went inside the building, along marble corridors and sun-drenched courtyards - fourteen in all. We climbed up the stairs to look at Diego Rivera's frescos. This extraordinary Mexican painter spent his life painting the history of his country, condemning not only the Spaniards, but also the Church and the Government. He painted until his death fifteen years ago from cancer. He was unable to complete his frescos. They have remained unfinished, since no painter seemed fit to take up his brush. He gave his labour free and was not paid for this particular work.

Our Mexican guide was marvellous. By choosing these frescos, he brought the turbulent past of his country alive for us. He started way back with some of the original tribes. There were 68 in all, with their own customs, their own language, their own culture. He told us about their customs. He explained the famous Ball Game, the forerunner of basketball, played between two tribes as a religious ritual. He spoke about the Dance of the Flying Birdman. Taxes were already known in the times of the Aztecs and paid with coffee beans. Prostitution was accepted as the only way widows could survive.

We saw the fresco depicting the founding of Mexico City, known as Tenochtilan City, in the centre of a vast lake. Here the Tenocheas (later called Aztecs) found an eagle perched on a prickly pear tree, holding a serpent in his talons. This was the omen, which had been foretold, indicating the site of the future capital. Ingeniously, the bridges built of wood, which led across the lake to the city, could be drawn up in times of danger. These surely were the prototypes for the future drawbridges.

We passed on to the times of Cortes and saw the cruelty and viciousness of those days. Cortes himself was a caricature of a man with an evil face and grossly swollen knees. Apparently, Cortes' skeleton was found in the Old Hospital of Jesu. Rivera took his measurements from this and found evidence of tuberculosis, syphilis and arthritis.

We retraced our steps and looked at the enormous mural over the staircase. We listened as the whole panorama of history unfolded before us, starting with the 'God of the Feathered Serpent' or Quetzalcoatl. The story goes that once upon a time, a white man with blue eyes and a red beard appeared on the shores of Mexico. Possibly he was a shipwrecked Viking. He taught the Olmecs many things about agriculture and husbandry. They worshipped him like a god. He disappeared, but was found in other parts of Mexico. The Olmecs elevated him to a god and named him Quetzalcoatl, God of the Feathered Serpent.

We followed Rivera through all the hardships of the Spanish Conquest, of greed and avarice, of revolution, inquisition, counter-revolution, of the tragic times of Maximilian, the ill-fated regent appointed by the French, and Carlotta, his wife. We followed Rivera to the fight for freedom, demonstrated by Mexico's heroes, such as the priest Hildalgo, who rang the Freedom Bell to summon everyone to fight for independence. We perceived Rivera's vision of Communism for Mexico.

The initial impression of this massive mural is one of confusion and ugliness, until you find the key and suddenly it becomes coherent and rather moving.

We emerged into bright sunshine and found the Plaza crowded with many tourists. We went down the Metro, of which the Mexicans are justly proud, all marble and beautifully clean. No graffiti disfigures the walls, no refuse sullies the shining floors. This way we crossed the square to emerge in front of the cathedral, the largest Catholic church in the world. Known as the Cathedral of the Annunciation, it is the metropolitan cathedral of all Mexico. Impressive, forming a wholeness of design, in spite of the use of various styles of architecture. Within it has numerous altars - nineteen, I think. We concentrated on the Altar of the Crucifix of the Poison, with its black Christ nailed to the cross. Legend has it that a bishop had many enemies. He was wont to kiss the feet of this crucifix every day. His enemies placed poison on the soles of Christ to send him to his certain death. Each time he bent to kiss the feet, they withdrew from his lips, absorbing all the poison and turning the image of Christ black.

We saw a woman with plastic curlers in her hair, saying her prayers. Later, we saw many women in public places with large pink and blue curlers in their hair, and came to the conclusion that this was the fashion in Mexico at this particular time.

The main altar, the Altar of the Four Kings, is all in heavy 24

View of Mexico City from our hotel.

Olmec sculpture.

carat gold leaf, covering carved red cedar wood. This is the contribution of a Spanish nobleman, who never set foot on Mexican soil. The style is 'Churringuesque', which is basically baroque, but even more elaborate, peculiar to Mexico. It bears the name of the architect whose work it was originally. There were also paintings on the altar. Dark, dark paintings, set amongst all the gold, executed by a self-taught Mexican painter by the name of Trivero.

We slipped into the sacristy, which houses some lovely paintings and beautifully carved chairs around a superb refectory table. There was a particularly charming painting of Madonna and Child.

Adjacent to the cathedral stands the 'Sagrario', a chapel built in local stone with an extraordinarily ornate facade. Both churches are visibly subsiding. We stepped into the Sagrario and found the interior strangely at variance with its facade, extremely simple and austere.

We quickly glanced at the imposing frontage of the National Pawnshop across the square, before we climbed on our little bus. We drove through an elegant shopping street, regaining the Paseo de la Reforma and following the stream of apparently orderly traffic, past now familiar landmarks, and reached Chapultepec Park with its castle perched on top of 'Grasshopper Hill'. This castle, which at one time was a military school and later served as palace for the Emperor Maximilian and his Carlotta, is now the History Museum. Six young cadets defended the castle in 1874 against U.S.A. troops and threw themselves to certain death from the castle roof, preferring death to captivity. A colossal monument at the entrance of the park commemorates this event. One column for each boy soldier soars up into the sky.

It is a lovely park with many beautiful trees. The Indians bring their families here on Sundays and on holidays to picnic on the grass. Inside the park stand many monuments. The Mexicans excel in this. There are also gifts from other nations, such as the Totem Pole from Canada, a pagoda from Vietnam, and a statue of Winston Churchill from Great Britain. The most important complex, however, is the museums area and the crowning glory of them all is the National

Museum of Anthropology. We passed the boating lake and the zoo and many eating places. We reached the end of the old part of the park and arrived at the President's official residence, known as 'Los Pinos'. We crossed a broad ring-road to enter the new part of the park. This is laid out with different shrubs, and has an enormous amusement park near the entrance, which our guide referred to as 'The Park of Mechanical Toys', where for a dollar a day all toys can be used. We stopped to take photographs of a hideous sculpture of the 'Raingod', lying prostrated on the ground. This too is one of Rivera's works. We also halted to admire a mosaic wall, well washed by fountains, forming the background of an enormous replica of sculptured heads of Olmecs.

We left the park and drove up to the Chapultepec Heights, which is a new residential quarter with some very beautiful villas and some very ornate residences. We noticed that almost everywhere the houses tend to 'cluster' close together, as if looking for support and shelter from each other.

We returned to the park and asked to be put down by the museum. We sat in the sun at the lakeside in one of the simple eating places. We each had a Torta, which is a tasty roll, and an orange juice. We watched the well-behaved youngsters enjoying 'snowcones', simple crumbled icecubes topped with sweet syrup. Betty and I tried Tacos, little squares of maize dough deep fried. I do not care too much for the hot chilli sauce the locals sprinkle on the tacos or the drop of lime juice. However, I always like to try unfamiliar dishes.

We crossed the busy road to visit the Museum of Anthropology. Outside, the massive monolith of Tlalos, the Raingod, is most impressive, forming a well-known landmark. The building itself was interesting, having been constructed around a central patio with a parasol roof, which is supported by an enormous carved column. There were twenty three rooms. Thirteen, situated on the ground floor, are devoted to archaeology, the remaining twelve on the first floor to ethnography. We spent our time in the most beautifully set out archaeological section. The first rooms are an introduction to the earliest times, depicting fossils and the evolution of man. Later, the rooms are arranged into specific areas and into the various tribes of Mexico. Each room is subdivided into chronological eras. We were amazed at the wealth of stone images. We saw the gruesome sacrificial stone and the famous 'Biedre de Sol', the Sun Stone, which is the Aztec Calendar Stone. In the Aztec section we became familiar with the Sacred Feathered Serpent, depicted in all kinds of positions.

Time was far too short to do justice to all the exhibits. We hoped to return to browse again and also visit the ethnographic section. We stepped out into the sun-drenched patio, casting a last look back to the peaceful pond with reeds and water-lilies, receiving its water from the big sculptured shell outside the Aztec Pavilion.

We crossed the park in search of Calle Dante to call on a friend of a friend of Betty's. We asked and set off in the direction given to us. We asked again and were offered a lift, which seemed easier than trying to explain. The man in question, a chemical engineer, working for Merk, did not speak English and none of us spoke Spanish. We were in the quarter of poets and writers and passed through Calle Victor Hugo, before we finally reached our destination.

We entered through the garage into a very cool and dark reception room, rather mid-European in decor and furniture. The lady of the house was Mexican, married to an Englishman. He had been a well known tennis player in his younger years. He quickly disappeared. We were joined by a young English P.G., who was engaged to a Mexican. It was interesting to talk to our hostess. She appeared a very forthright person, asking pertinent questions and giving us a quick resume of her family history, back to her grandfather. We sipped lemon tea and ate fruitcake. When we took our leave, Carmen, our hostess, insisted on accompanying us, intent on showing us Hotel Camino Real. Their car was out of action so we went on foot to the hotel, wondering why she was so keen on taking us there.

It turned out to be an amazing place, built in 1968 for the Olympic Games. The courtyard contained a pool which was in continuous motion, simulating the sea, and lit up at night in ever-changing colours. The whole building was palatial with many reception rooms, conference halls, restaurants, arcades of elegant shops and swimming pools. There are a number of murals, executed by modern Mexican painters. Pedro Friedberg is one of them. His paintings display geometric forms in an exercise of true perspective. Another painter by the name of Tamoya presented a brilliantly coloured jungle scene in the 'Naive Style'. On leaving this amazing complex, we had great difficulties in finding a taxi in the neverending stream of traffic. Eventually we managed to get one and bade farewell to our hostess. We returned to our hotel, well content with our day.

Yesterday we set off in the morning and drove once again along the Paseo de la Reforma, out of town. All along the road were altars, about thirteen of them. Pilgrims on the way to the Shrine of the Lady of Guadalupe stop at these altars as they walk along. According to a legend the Virgin Mary appeared to a poor Indian boy at this special spot. She entrusted him with a message to the Bishop to build a shrine. Three times did she appear to Juan Diego and three times he asked the Bishop, who sent him away. Eventually the Bishop asked for a miracle. It was December. When Juan returned once more to the bare hilltop, he found a garden of sweet-smelling roses. The simple boy picked the roses, and hiding them beneath his sarap, he hurried to the Bishop. When he opened his sarap, the imprint of the Virgin Mary was plainly visible. The Virgin of Guadalupe is dark skinned and therefore most venerated by all Indians. The Metropolitan Cathedral in the Zocalo of Mexico City may be the official cathedral of Mexico, but the Shrine of Guadalupe is the true church belonging to every Mexican. This is a vast complex of churches, but one by one the churches have subsided and can no longer be used. A new modern church has been built, but is not yet complete. It is round, with a curious, almost sail-like roof. People come from all corners of Mexico. Many approach upon their knees up the steep stone steps across the vast plaza. The dark Indians ride into town for miles, tethering their little horses to a special wooden post behind the church. Inside, the church made a somewhat gaudy impression on us. The floor is beautiful, cool Mexican marble. Red Cedar wood is used in the surrounding hall and glittering lamps hang suspended from the ceiling. Many floral tributes are brought daily by the pilgrims to be placed near the altar. The image of the Lady of Guadalupe stands above the altar, below a heavy gold crown. We descended into the crypt to glance up at her lovely face. A 'rolling carpet' is planned, to enable the large number of worshippers to see their 'Indita', their 'Little Indian'.

We spent some time browsing in the big government-controlled art and craft shop, displaying some of their excellent ware in silver, onyx, horn, leather, etc. We bought a very elegant chess set in horn. These transactions are a trifle tedious, since Mexicans are never in a hurry. Finally, we were on our way again and passed the city boundaries, which are marked by two 'Green Indians', statues of two warriors made in copper, covered by patina.

We continued our journey through flat and arid country. Barren soil lay between spiky cactus plants. Little congregations of houses appeared now and again, all with flat roofs bearing watertanks. Some were mere shacks, others certainly belonged to well-to-do city people with cars in front of their houses. There is an industrial estate just beyond the city boundaries. Squatters' hovels climb up the hill behind the new community. As always, these habitations were nestling close together. We passed an enormous monastery, the biggest in all Mexico. It is being restored and will be opened as a museum in the future. We reached the famous site of the Pyramids of Teotihuaca at long last. Unfortunately, it was very windy and a sandstorm blew up. Because of these conditions, we decided against ascending these enormous pyramids, realising that the view would be completely shrouded by dust. The vast complex has been almost completely reconstructed. We could appreciate the general layout easily. In parts we could still see the original floor and some of the entrancing carvings of the well preserved, famous 'Plumed Serpent', Quetzalcoatl. These four-sided, terraced pyramids were temples - the sacrifices took place in front of them. The vast complex - as far as archaeologists could interpret - consisted of a citadel, an avenue with temples to either side and the two main structures facing each other, the Pyramid of the Sun opposite the Pyramid of the Moon. Many bones have been found in the smaller temples and hence the avenue has been named 'The Street of the Dead'.

Time allotted was short. We therefore set off on our own to find some well preserved wall paintings in some of the many palaces adjacent to the temples. They were quite exquisite, particularly in Jaguars' Palace, with jaguars depicted in various guises. The mural in the main room shows cats with human heads. The last set of rooms in the great courtyard contain frescos of giant jaguars wearing Egyptian-looking head-dresses. They are blowing on sea-shells and sound glyphs are issuing forth. Small holes in the floors here and there are part of the drainage system, which still functions after a thousand years. To reach the Palace of the Jaguars, we had to enter the Palace of Butterflies, which is almost completely reconstructed and shows the layout of the palace complex. Built around a central courtyard, the rooms are dark. All light enters from the patio, which is surrounded by a pillared portico, evocative of Knossos.

A tunnel under the Butterfly Palace led us to an earlier palace. This had been filled in to act as base for the later Butterfly Palace. The method of using one building as a base for a later one is frequently used for temples and palaces alike. The paintings in the Shell Palace are beautiful and well preserved. The background of the temple portico is painted deep red and other colours are used to depict a series of shells, decorated with feathers, flowers, and green birds with yellow beaks.

As a special treat our guide took us to Tepantilla behind the Pyramid of the Sun, which has some remnants of exquisite murals of the Raingod Tlalos, with water dropping from his hands onto small human figures, frolicking in gardens. The second mural is of the famous Ball Game. The colours, blue, red, yellow and brown, are remarkably fresh and vivid and have maintained their original shades. We left reluctantly, having succumbed and bought a small obsidian figure of a god from the little boys who seem to be an intricate part of this ancient site.

After an excellent Mexican meal, we drove back to the city. Far on the horizon, we were able to see both Popocatepetel ('Popo' for short) and Iztaccithuatl, with their snow-capped peaks.

The nephew of a very dear patient of mine had been living in Mexico for the past year. He had contacted me and we arranged to meet after our return from Teotihuacan. He arrived soon after we got back to our hotel and drove us out of town, past the familiar landmarks of the statue of Charles 4th of Spain, known as 'El Caballito', which means the 'Little Horse', Christopher Columbus, the noble figure of Cuahtemac, the last Aztec Emperor, to the Monument of Independence with its eternal flame, crowned by a golden angel. We skirted the Chapultepec Park, noting once again the horrific monolith of the Raingod outside the National Museum of Anthropology. We climbed up through the heights of Chapultepec, leaving expensive, elegant residences behind us. We came to his home in a new estate around a ravine. The house stands in splendid isolation high above the smog of the city. Francis works for the British Council in connection with student grants. His young wife Isobel copes with the house and their three children. The house is quite modern, on three levels, with various small patios and gardens. Lovely, delicate orchids abound, suspended from small pieces of wood bark. Lucy's (she is aged ten, but looks older than her years) white pet rabbit has made short shrift of any flowers in the top garden and the newly acquired chickens help to make a thorough job of it. We were proudly shown an enormous sunken bath. Alas, the water pressure is too poor, so it is seldom used.

The two other children are Peter, aged five, and Sally, who is three and a half and very bright. Lucy, like her mother, feels the difficulty of isolation, probably due to lack of communication. Francis speaks Spanish and the two younger children have picked it up easily. In any case, Peter and Sally are good companions, and are content. The family have a maid, a young, mini-skirted girl from a small village. The maids start their day's work with cleaning the cars and thus meet up first thing in the morning for a good gossip. They all water their employer's gardens. The rest of the day is spent doing housework. Saturday night they spend their time with friends, returning Sunday night. They return to their families for their holidays and find it difficult to break away from this strong tie.

It is a strange life for this young couple, who have spent most of their married life abroad. Starting in Sierra Leone, then to Kuwait and Somalia. I found it interesting to talk to Francis. He realises that this kind of life puts a heavy burden on his wife and places enormous strain on their marriage. Families are very isolated. The children go to British schools, Isobel goes into town once a week to shop in one of the supermarkets. I wonder how they will settle down to life in Britain when the time comes for them to return.

Francis compared the corruptibility of the police in the various places of the world he had been to. In Somalia, a Muslim country, the police are incorruptible. The same went for the Bedouins in Kuwait. In Sierra Leone, a Christian country, the police were frighteningly corrupt. He did point out, in all fairness, that the police in Mexico are so poorly paid that they could not exist without relying on bribes. This is an accepted way of life in Mexico. Franics also mused about the clash between the Indians and Spaniards. A confrontation of two equally cruel and brutal nations. I would have liked to have more opportunity for serious conversation.

Both Francis and Isobel were extremely hospitable. It must have been quite tedious to entertain three complete strangers. Isobel offered to meet us again, before we left Mexico, and to show us some of the sites which we had missed. As the sun set, we had a superb view of both 'Popo' and Iztaccithuatl glowing in pink hues.

It was still early when we returned to our hotel. We slipped out into the street again, making for Garibaldi Plaza. We mingled with the crowd, walked past the innumerable poor Indians who were squatting on the pavement, offering their wares or simply begging. A harrowing sight. These people are incredibly poor and illness must be rampant amongst them. They are truly pathetic.

Wherever we went in Mexico lottery tickets were being offered. This is a nationalized institution. As in the East, food is available on the street at all hours, day and night. It is freshly cooked and eaten on the spot. I think, as in the East, most people have no cooking facilities at home, and food is relatively cheap to buy, tacos and tortillas costing very little. Both are made from maize flour. Tacos are fried, tortillas are shaped into rounds, flattened between two boards and baked on a griddle. Hot chilli sauce is sprinkled on both and many different fillings are used for the tortillas, which are then rolled up daintily to be eaten with your fingers.

We were carried along by the crowd, past a 'fire eater', who did not have an audience at all, past a couple of balloon sellers with an astonishing number of those colourful bubbles. We finally arrived at the square, where many musicians had assembled. They were dressed in black flared trousers studded with silver, white shirts and black waistcoats also with silver studs. Their black sombreros were similarly adorned. There are numerous groups of musicians, who all will serenade anyone willing to listen and willing to pay. Around the square are many restaurants. Many tourists find their way to Garibaldi Plaza later in the evening, to eat and to be serenaded. In one corner stands an enormous hall, if indeed one can call this ramshackle building thus. The noise, the smell, the acrid smoke from all the open charcoal fires and grills is quite indescribable. The place was full of people eating, talking and being serenaded. This amazing spectacle is a nightly event.

Sunday morning saw us on our way to Xochimilco (pronounced 'Socomilco'). We stopped At Sullivan Park at the outskirts of town, a pretty little park with an attractive abstract sculpture in the centre and a modern church with lovely stained glass windows on one side. The aspiring artists exhibited here every Sunday. We strolled along in the sunshine. Some of the paintings were very good indeed and Betty presented us with an extremely pleasant picture. In fact, we have two pictures mounted side by side within one frame. One is a picture of Tasco, the Silver Town, the other is a Mexican woman. We are extremely pleased with it and it will be hung next to our Tibetan drawings. Ruth also purchased one of their very attractive rugs in white and brown, depicting the Mexican eagle on the cactus tree, devouring the snake. She was particularly pleased with herself since she offered half the starting price and this was accepted, just as we were boarding our bus again.

We soon reached the highway, having passed a cinema with a colourful mosaic by Rivera. This illustrates the development of Mexican art. The cinema plays an important part in the life of the Mexican people, since it is the cheapest form of entertainment. We passed the university complex, catching a glimpse of the world-famous mosaics which cover the entire library building.

We stopped outside the town and there, on our right, we saw the tall red buildings of the Olympic Village, looking picturesque against the deep green backcloth of trees at the foot of the now burnt-out volcano known as 'Xitle, Umbelicus'. On our left was Cuicuilco, the oldest pyramid, entirely round in shape and not reconstructed. The new and the old, both on a bed of lava, make an interesting contrast. Once upon a time Xitle, like Vesuvius, covered the whole area with molten lava.

We passed the Aztec Stadium, built for the Olympic Games in 1968, and now used for soccer. It is pleasant to look at, like many of the official buildings in Mexico.

We reached the little town of Xochimilco, with attractive, colonial-style houses and a shady plaza with a big baroque church, which was decorated for a wedding. We continued to the little harbour with its many flat-bottomed craft bedecked with flowers. The Floating Islands no longer float. Initially these were man-made islands in the fresh water lake of Xochimilco, which were extremely fertile. They still supply all fruit and vegetables to the city. Since they did float originally, the occupants planted a special kind of willow tree, which is slender and therefore does not take up much valuable ground, but has a deep root, which acts as an anchor. The boats are used to convey fruit and vegetables to the shores in the early morning. Later, chairs and trestle tables are placed aboard for the tourists and the Mexican families. Alas, there are no longer flowers lining the canals, since people used to pick them all too readily. There was little life on the waters on the Sunday morning when we were there. Only few boats with families passed by, one or two floating restaurants glided past us, cooking tortillas or roasting corn on the cob. Few of the famous bands serenaded on this sunny day. One boat, offering orchids, roses and humble violets, came alongside and another with rugs and shawls. We sampled a tequila cocktail, ate our picnic lunch and finally left the boat, which was immediately overrun by hordes of youngsters, scavenging for any leftovers.

Back in Mexico City, we decided to stroll out again, mixing with the locals. In a little square we found 'San Fernando', a lovely church, crowded with worshippers. Once again I was touched by the sincerity and devotion of ordinary people. It reminded me very much of my very good Spanish friend, who will start off any anniversary, such as her wedding day, by going to church to give thanks for yet another happy year. We walked through many back streets until we reached the 'Pink Zone', where all the international restaurants are situated. We looked for a travel bureau, which we found, to ascertain what trips we could undertake on our return to Mexico City from our tour to the Yucatan.

Later that evening, we dressed up in our best bib and tucker and walked across Alameda Park to the Palace de Belles Artes to watch Folkloric.

The building itself is on a very grand scale, all cool marble with numerous auditoria, concert halls and galleries for exhibitions. The performance was absolutely charming. There was little Indian dancing, but extremely attractive French, Spanish and true Mexican dances from various regions of Mexico, performed in colourful, traditional costumes to music with a rhythmic beat.

We walked back through the balmy night, past courting couples in Alameda Park.

Next morning, the three of us set off bright and early to explore Mexico City on foot. We walked leisurely in the warm sunshine, looking for churches, which are all open during the day and where we could, step in to walk round quietly. The people who come to pray, seemed oblivious of our presence. Almost every church we visited contained a grandfather clock somewhere near the altar, showing the correct time, which struck us as rather odd.

We walked past closed shops. I do not think that life really starts before 11 am, except the traffic. Although we had thought that traffic runs quietly and smoothly, walking around we realised that a large number of accidents occur every day. By now we had become accustomed to the almost continuous wail of the ambulances, night and day. We reached the Zocalo and spent a fascinating time in the Official Pawnshop, which occupies a grand building. After six months any object not redeemed is offered for sale to the public. The number of articles and variety of goods for sale was astonishing.

We sat on the sunny square to decide on our next step, then

set off to stroll through narrow thoroughfares to the charming old square of Santo Domingo. A hundred years ago, public scribes sat under the arcades on the west side, since most people were unable to read or write. Some fifty typists have succeeded and are kept very busy all day long. We stepped into the fine baroque church of Santo Domingo with its graceful tower and an ornate Churriquesque altar. We looked briefly into the simple, smaller church nearby, before continuing our walk through a graceful archway right into the slums of Mexico. The streets were narrow, the poverty and dirt were quite appalling. Some of the houses were very lovely and well proportioned, built in the old colonial style.

We ambled back to Santo Domingo Square and entered the sunny courtyard of the Old Medical School, later the dreaded House of Inquisition, and now serving as the Faculty for Gynaecology and Obstetrics. 'Nature called' and we found a suitable and convenient student's cloakroom to avail ourselves. Somebody approached Ruth to ask her her business. She quickly explained that she was waiting for the doctor. We walked up the splendid staircase to admire the remains of an old marble mosaic and looked down into the courtyard, where students were earnestly discussing their work. We slowly retraced our steps back to the Zocalo, past many old buildings - most of them schools or offices of the Ministry of Education. We marvelled at the many small workshops in the narrow sidestreets, before passing on to look for somewhere to eat and to rest our weary feet. We joined the locals in a big, cool, old-fashioned eating place and had great fun in choosing our menu without being able to communicate verbally. We did not do too badly, finishing off with oyster cocktail, taco with bean paste, topped with local cheese and some delicious flat fish, fried. All this washed down with local beer made a splendid meal. Refreshed, we wandered on, back through Alameda Park. We wondered at the great number of public telephones all along the streets. Truly public, since they have only a plastic shell to grant privacy. They are very much in use. The other fact which amazed us was the absence of smoking in the street. Smoking is prohibited in all public places.

We went again to a bank to change money. One is more palatial than the next. All cool marble, without grills, all business is conducted across the open counter. We slowly made our way back to the hotel, noting that many shops were highly decorated in readiness for St. Valentine's Day. We had not known that this day was celebrated as it is in England with appropriate cards and gifts. It certainly was not known on the Continent in the past.

By midday it had become extremely hot. We left Betty to rest in the hotel and set off on our own. We strolled through a craft shop, attached to a museum for handicraft, which alas was closed. All museums are shut on Mondays. We stopped for an excellent cup of coffee in an all-male coffee bar, before sallying forth in search of the Plaza of the Three Cultures. By now we were rather footweary and extremely hot, so we took the Metro and found this a very simple operation. Only one rate existed for all journeys, you surrendered your ticket at the turnstile as you go through. The carriages are French-built and run smoothly and noiselessly on rubber tyres.

It was a fair step from the Metro station to the Plaza, through a modern housing estate. The site, which lies below ground level at the foot of the old Spanish church of Santiago Tlataclo, is the original heart of the Aztec city and is beautiful, with a number of pyramids, walls and pavements. The church itself is baroque, with a surprisingly simple interior, with blue light filtering through stained glass windows. The effigy of the saint in its glass coffin looks incredibly lifelike. We did not know whether it was a wax image or an embalmed body. We sat for a little while in the adjacent sun-drenched cloisters, before wandering back again.

We passed the very modern hospital of the new estate. Most villages have a 'modern clinic', a fact which we had noticed on our various excursions. We decided to hail a taxi to take us to the travel office, which was right in town. In Mexico City, you either see large, American-type cars, or small cars such as Volkswagen, which are often used as taxis. We had a cheerful driver who spoke a modicum of English. Our business completed, we walked slowly back to our hotel. After a bath and change of clothes, we were taken to a special Mexican restaurant for a typical local meal. The restaurant was crowded with parties of every nationality, with a preponderance of

French Canadians. It was extremely noisy, but the food was intriguing. It is one of the entertainments offered to tourists and one has to accept graciously so as not to offend.

We set off on our trip next morning with our ultimate goal being Yucatan. We travelled along the high road, which is a toll road. There was a good deal of heavy traffic outside Mexico City. By our standards, the Mexicans do not drive fast.

We passed through poor neighbourhoods on the outskirts of the town. Now and again amidst the little flat-roofed shacks, a watertank rose into the sky. We were told that the people living on the estate decide on the necessity for such a tank and then approach the authorities, willing to bear half the cost. The local council will install the tank and the community pays the rest. We started climbing. On the lower hills, political slogans appeared. These will be changed when the present President departs and a new one begins his term of office.

Unfortunately the sky remained overcast, though we did manage to glimpse the two volcanoes - Popo and The Sleeping Woman. The countryside looked rather arid and sparsely populated, yet we were assured that this was arable land; that it was 'resting time' for the fields just now. Soon planting would commence: corn and beans, their staple food, would be sown amongst the fruit trees. This combination was found to enhance all three crops. This fact has no scientific explanation. We left the fields behind and reached the wooded regions. Once again, our guide was able to add interest by his explanation that anyone desiring to cut down one tree was obliged to plant seven new ones. In former days Mexico was rich in forestry, but this has been sadly depleted for shipbuilding and other constructions, hence this new law was passed and put into operation.

We passed through dusty villages, on a detour to visit the archaeological site at Cholula, which always reminded us of 'shanty towns at the outpost of the Empire'. We came past the oldest monastery to the site. Wherever you find a monastery anywhere in Mexico, rest assured there will be an ancient city nearby.

Cholula has many beautiful churches, since Cortes promised to build a church for every pyramid he razed to the ground. Spires and multi-coloured cupolae shimmered in the far distance as we approached the city. Legend has it that the Toltecs founded the town. Quetzalcoatl, the first white man, stayed here for twenty years and taught the people about agriculture, husbandry science and art, before departing towards the Gulf of Mexico. He left four disciples behind, promising to return, whilst they continued his work. When later the Spaniards arrived, the Toltecs did not initially offer any resistance, thinking that Quetzalcoatl had returned. Cortes was also fair-skinned with a red beard. Strange that the Indians too should be waiting for the return of the Messiah.

Our guide explained that the Toltecs, although they were very cruel indeed, had already achieved civilisation. They had devised a precise calendar and were well versed in medicine and surgery. So much for civilisation, may it be in the times of the Toltecs or our own! But let me return to the site, which is truly magnificent. Here you find the biggest pyramid and excavation still continues. Following our guide, we entered a warren of underground passages. It was most interesting - at intervals, on the right and the left, were steps and drainage and other channels from previous periods. In fact, to date, eight levels have been excavated. The largest part of the pyramid cannot be exposed, since one of Cortes' churches stands on the top. Unfortunately we had no time to visit any of the churches. We emerged from the tunnel at the back of the pyramid into bright sunshine. We glanced across to more churches in the distance. We looked at some old walls and some of the original floor. We saw some decorated clay vessels and some skeletons which had been found and left in situ. We admired an old stele and an enormous stone head next to an ancient figure of the famous jaguar. We saw two different types of drainage systems. A very old one, where bottomless urns were ingeniously inserted into each other, and the later more familiar one of open stone gutters. On reaching the front of the pyramid we saw the oldest part, build of adobe, sun-baked mud brick.

We returned to Cholula, which has a railway line and many attractive colonial houses, and from here travelled further towards the Gulf of Mexico, passing through the outskirts of Pueblo, which is famous for its tiles. The district which we saw looked modern and rather prosperous. It is a large town, lying in a fertile area. Apple orchards surround the town and sidar or Mexican Apple champagne is produced in Pueblo State.

We drove past haciendas. These used to be the equivalent of our manor houses with large grounds and belonged to the very rich. New ones were being built, but they had much less ground, although it was well cultivated. Now and again conical, white silos appeared in the landscape. They are used to store grain.

We passed women laundering their garments in small streams using stones, as it was done in olden days. Turkeys arrived on the scene, strutting proudly about. They, of course, originated in Mexico. We were still in the state of Pueblo. We were to pass through many of Mexico's 31 states on our journey. We were told that the road we took that day was a most wonderful, scenic route. Unfortunately we had no view at all, once we reached the pass of Cumbres, 2,515 metres above the sea, fog descended. All I can say is, that we travelled on a wonderful mountain road with numerous curves, through the forests, down into the valley of Veracruz. We continued through a wide valley surrounded by a magnificent view of mountains, with the majestic volcano Citalteple, also known as Pico de Orizaba, amongst them. It is an extinct volcano, and is the third highest mountain in Mexico. Alas, once again clouds soon obscured the snow-capped top. The landscape grew more lush and trees appeared. We had seen palm trees lining the avenues in Mexico City. These were date palms, which never bear fruit. Outside Mexico City were many eucalyptus trees. They are natives of Australia, but have become well established in Mexico.

We were approaching Cordoba, which boasts the best coffee in Mexico. (We did, however, not see any plantations, since they lie beyond the hills which we glimpsed in the distance.) It is a pretty little village with narrow streets, lined by white painted houses with wooden balconies and windows protected by grilles, with overhanging roofs to give shade. We stopped in the square. Every town and village in Mexico has a square and a church. The square with four important buildings, either temples or palaces in each corner, formed part of every ancient site. Strange, how traditions linger on. The parish church stands on Cordoba's main square. Opposite rises the former Casas Reales, now the Palacia Municipale. The remaining two sides have some splendid colonial buildings with projecting roofs and balconies. In the cool shade of arcades are many little restaurants. Here we ate a simple meal in true Mexican style and bought true Mexican coffee to take back with us.

With just a few minutes to spare, we paid a quick visit to the church. I was intrigued to find the figure of Christ carrying the cross clothed in purple velvet. Many silver votives were pinned on the robe. A small open coffin contained the figure of a much venerated saint. The face, bearing a most agonised expression, was exposed - the rest of the figure covered by snow white lace.

We had descended quite rapidly to reach Cordoba and found ourselves in the Tropics. Mango trees appeared for the first time. They are beautiful trees, round in shape, with dense foliage of red and green. Some were in flower. There were banana plantations of many varieties, small ones known as finger bananas, purple and red ones and one particularly hard type, which is only used as cattle food. We passed pineapple plantations and coconut palm groves, well cultivated in this part of Mexico. There were many trees bearing brilliant flowers, such as Poinsettia (named after a French botanist), which are native to Mexico. Tulip trees and lush Bougainvillaea and many which we did not know, as for instance a wild tree bearing golden flowers. There were few birds, but many lovely butterflies and blackbirds with golden-tipped wings. Sugar-cane seemed to be everywhere, either growing or cut and neatly piled on lorries which passed by. Before cutting, the outside leaves are burnt to free them from snakes and insects, since cutting is done by hand.

Quite suddenly - it seemed to me - we had reached the ocean and found ourselves at the outskirts of Veracruz, the most important port of Mexico, which was our first stop for the night.

The roads were lined by small flat-roofed villas and a number of hotels. We drove past harbours, one for small boats, the other for container boats. Sandy beaches shimmered like silver along the ocean. We reached the promenade and our hotel, opposite the Fort of San Juan, which even today looks sinister with its thick, crenellated walls.

At one stage during the War of Independence it had been used as a prison, and prisoners had been subjected to 'water torture'. Except for this bleak, forbidding building, the town made a light and gay impression. We walked along the narrow streets between ancient houses. Bars with stable-doors intrigued us. Some living quarters looked barely habitable. We were impressed by a most beautiful tiled house on the main square, now a very elegant 'House of Haute Couture' with a tiled staircase leading up to the first floor. Close to it stands Parroquie, the Cathedral. A service was in progress, we quietly slipped in and out again, but I noticed impressive wood carvings of the hands of Christ signifying the Stations of the Cross.

The rest of the square was lined by bars, restaurants and coffee shops. We sat down amongst the local population, sipping tequila, licking salt and sucking lime, as the Mexicans do. Tequila is their local drink, prepared from the ubiquitous cactus plant. We were serenaded by various musicians, who moved with their xylophone-like instruments from one little bar to another, hoping to collect some pesos, bursting into song spontaneously. We had had this experience at Cordoba, when we were having lunch in the square. It was a balmy night and extremely pleasant to sit and watch the people around us and see children playing in a little park in the centre of the square.

We strolled back to our hotel through yet another warren of little cobbled streets and alleyways and stopped at the many small shops along the waterfront, finally purchasing a shopping basket. Basketwork, using sisal, is a very ancient craft used in these parts. After an excellent meal we walked out once more, along the promenade, past courting couples and watched darkness descend over the sea.

We watched the Navy hoist the Mexican flag at the Naval Institute adjacent to our hotel next morning before we set off on our long journey to Villahermosa. This was an extremely leisurely affair, with both young women and young men attending in their white uniforms.

The roads were mostly straight with the 'sleeping policemen' - similar to our cattle grids - outside towns and villages, to slow down traffic. The countryside was mainly flat with big cattle ranches.

We criss-crossed the big river Grijavla, with marshland either side. We had arrived in the province of Tabasco. Tabasco means 'Wet Land'. We were told that this area is infested with snakes and alligators. Our journey took us past oil-fields and oil plants; we saw neither snakes nor alligators. Tabasco is a wealthy state, producing coffee, tobacco, vanilla, cocoa, spices, sugar and rubber. Chicle is grown near Villahermosa. Villahermosa means 'Fair City'. We saw big wooden buildings, where tobacco leaves were being dried, whilst Mexican cowboys, beneath their broad-brimmed hats, tended their horses, cows and zebus (known as sebus in Mexico). The soil in Tabasco was not the black, volcanic type we had seen on the High Plateau, but red, presumably with a high iron content. The houses here in the tropic were different too, mainly wooden shacks with thatched roofs, reminiscent of Africa.

Most of the bigger villages had modern 'Rural Schools' at the outskirts. In theory, all children had to go to school. In practice, many children did not attend regularly, since they are needed to help at home.

We stopped near a lake and wandered off the highway into a small village. A boy had slung his hammock between two palm trees for his midday rest. Children came running out of poor huts and shyly gaped at us. Mothers stood holding their babies and stared at our strange features in amazement. But they did not mind being photographed.

We arrived hot and sticky at the town of Villahermosa. Driving along the main avenue, we reached the banks of the river Grijavla and retraced our steps, passing the cathedral, which looked impressive from the distance, with its twin towers. However, it was in the process of being rebuilt and at present only the towers were complete. We arrived at our hotel on the outskirts of the city. A modern building, tastefully set around a cool courtyard full of tropical plants, kept cool by a fountain.

Our room overlooked a pond. It was peaceful and pleasant to stand and watch the graceful white birds (Egrets), which our guide called 'Little Storks'. Peace reigned until nightfall. A boat with a pipeline lay anchored in the middle of the pond . I do not know what purpose it all served, but when night fell the silence was shattered by the infernal noise of an engine, continuing its diabolic rhythm until the early hours of the morning.

The only two reasons for stopping overnight at this particular spot were, that firstly there was no other suitable hotel to break the journey, and more important, the 'Parque la Venta'. An expedition in 1925 had discovered huge sculptures depicting animals, humans, half-tiger, half-man, urns and altars in La Venta jungle, some 96 km from Villahermosa. These are now set amongst shady trees in a small park next to the hotel. We felt we were entering the jungle. It was incredibly humid and insects abounded. Having been forewarned, we were forearmed.

The sculptures were immensely impressive and are remnants from the Olmecs, a culture which flourished about 1154-174 BC. There were enormous heads displaying both Negroid and Mongoloid features. The origin of the Indians is much disputed, but because of the mixture of Negroid and Mongoloid traits found in these sculptures, many scientists think that they came from Asia. When we saw our first Indians in Mexico City, they reminded us of the Lapps in Swedish Lapland and of the Tibetans in Ladakh, with their broad faces, flat noses and slanting eyes. The faces in La Venta had thick eyebrows, broad noses, which were really the end-on views of the snake's face. The mouth was curved down, reminiscent of the tiger's (or jaguar's) fangs. Later sculptures showed teeth between their fleshy lips. The heads were covered with helmet-like structures, extending downwards in front of the ears, denoting that the Olmecs had been great warriors. Some of these massive heads were quite delightful, giving the impression of a round baby face. Some of the sculptures immortalising an event were most magnificent. Amongst this thick jungle, amidst these awe-inspiring monuments lived real animals found in the Tabasco Jungle. Cuddly little monkeys swung in the trees, alligators made use of the pools. In fact, we mistook one of these monsters, lying asleep on a rock, for a sculpture. Wild pigs and Jaguars also inhabited the park.

I hope that the photographs of these unique sculptures will come out, in spite of the absence of bright light. It was dark beneath the thick canopy of old trees.

There was a third reason for stopping at Villahermosa: a visit to Campeche to see 'Palenque'. I had been disappointed by the Pyramids of Tectihuacan, but thrilled by Cholula. 'Palenque' made me catch my breath and look in absolute enchantment. We drove past the village of the same name right into the jungle. In front of us rose the massive Pyramid of the Palace, whilst to our right innumerable stairs led up to the top of the enormous Pyramid of the Inscription. We climbed carefully to the top. The view across the many pyramids, with minor temples (some of these sadly dilapidated) set amongst the lushness of the jungle vegetation, was truly breathtaking. On top of the pyramid stood the Temple of Inscriptions. Called thus by archaeologists when they found a stone panel inside the temple, inscribed with 620 Hieroglyphs. Alas, no one has been able to decipher most of the scripts found here or elsewhere. Therefore, much of the past remains shrouded in mystery. More excitement was to follow. In 1925 a Mexican archaeologist solved the puzzle of certain round holes, covered with stone plugs, in two slabs of the temple floor. Many archaeologists had been bemused by them. Alberto Ruiz was able to remove the plugs and lift up the heavy slab. This opened up a staircase, which we descended. As we made our descent, the atmosphere grew colder and damper until we finally arrived at a chamber, which led to a vaulted tomb. It had been closed by an enormous rock, which could still be seen, pushed aside. Here, in front of our astonished eyes, stood the most beautiful sarcophagus. The top slab had been raised and lit up to illuminate the exquisite carving. The bottom slab contained the contours of a human body. Here, the archaeologists found the skeleton of the 'Man in the Jade Mask', still wearing jewellery, still showing traces of colour from the clothes he had worn. An exquisite statuette of the Sun God stood at his feet. Yet no one knows who this important man had been.

We ascended the majestic staircase of the palace, known as the Palace of the Counts, with its many rooms, which housed the highest priests in the hierarchy. Here we could appreciate the Mayan Arch, just seen in the Temple of Inscriptions. This in fact was not a true arch. It is the continuation of the walls, sturdily interlaced, without a keystone. It is generally known as the 'Corbel Arch' in architecture. We could see traces of stucco on exterior walls, with faint remnants of colour. In the courtyard stood the fragments of sculptures. We walked around the platform surrounding the Palace, and looked towards the East to more dilapidated temples on the tops of pyramids. One of these is called Temple of the Duke. A foreign duke is supposed to have lived within its walls for many years, venerated as a god by the local inhabitants - no doubt because of his fair skin. According to our guide, it was he who removed sculptures and votives from the temples and palaces to sell to the highest bidder. How else did many of the sculptures and votives reach museums as far afield as Vienna and had fallen into the hands of private collectors all over the world?

Next to the main buildings, which surrounded the courtyard, and which in their turn were surrounded by the aforesaid terrace, stood a square tower, probably used as a watch tower or for astronomy. We followed our guide through narrow corridors to the back of the main building and descended by a second stairway past an old altar. We crossed the clear little river Otulus, passed under a guava tree and some trees bearing sour oranges, which are used to enhance the flavour of beef, to reach the square. This was surrounded by four temples, each standing on top of a pyramid. We ascended the steps of the best preserved, the Temple of the Sun. The main body was extremely beautiful. Here we saw for the first time the sculptured image of Chaak, the Rain God. The altar was shaped in his image, with square eyes, broad nose, reminiscent of the serpent's nose, and drooping mouth and teeth, akin to the jaguar's fangs. We glanced across the square to the dilapidated Temple of the Cross, which still bore the Crestella, which literally translated means Cocks Comb, on top of the building. The Crestella consisted of a high wall with vertical slits which let the wind whistle through, and added height, without adding undue weight to the foundations.

We had time to wander between the ruins and to watch Indians scything the grass with stout machetes. I collected some wild flowers to bring home. We talked to a number of enterprising young people from America and Australia. They had been seeing Mexico the hard way. One couple, with a little girl on their back, had made their way by public transport.

We found a beautifully carved face on the East side of the wall of the Palace of the Counts. A young Indian was cleaning the sculpture adjacent to the human head. Patiently and gently, he removed the moss and lichen from the stone. We left this splendid site reluctantly to board our bus once more, for lunch. Sitting under a bamboo roof near a pool, we were served with a most delicious meal, Mayan style. Big pineapples and other fruit hung temptingly suspended from the roof. Our meal over, we watched local craftsmen fashioning stencils from original stone carvings, which we had just seen. These were then transferred onto leather and outlined with an electric needle. Some of the designs were sculpted by hand on limestone and sold as plaques. We bought some of the small ones, which were quite delightful.

We left Palanque, which lies in the State of Chiapas and formed the introduction to the Mayan Civilisation for us. We next entered the State of Campeche. It was a long and hot journey through tropical scenery. That night we stayed in a hotel, right on the shores of the Gulf of Mexico, built in splendid isolation, miles from anywhere. It resembled a Spanish Paradora. The original building had been part of an old hacienda with thick walls, cool halls and an imposing entrance. The furniture was in keeping with the era when the hacienda was first built. The rooms in an adjacent, modern, low house, pleasing to the eye and most comfortable - except none of the wash-basins was supplied with plugs, nor could we obtain such luxury anywhere. We had omitted to bring our universal plug. It was extremely humid and nothing would dry. I had a swim in the pool in the early morning and then a paddle in the warm but rather rough sea, before anybody was about.

We drove along the coast next morning to the fishing town of Campeche, which is the capital of the state. We had a little while to spare and were able to stroll round this pleasant town. We slipped into the church and into the adjacent courtyard, which was surrounded by old plaques. We peeped into the cool hall with its walls studded with hooks for fishing nets and returned to the sunny square.

Part of Campeche is very old with pink, blue, yellow and turquoise houses. We found a very old church, faced with multicoloured tiles, partly Byzantine in style. It was being renovated to be used as a library. Part of the stout sea wall, built to protect the town from pirates, was still intact and one of the proud gates still stood imposingly next to a modern complex of hotels, public buildings and a most attractive complex in the shape of a giant mushroom, which housed an auditorium on one side and a gallery displaying local craft on the other. Campeche seemed a pleasant place to linger for a little while. Apparently, the best shrimps are caught here. We noticed girls acting as traffic wardens. We had not seen this before.

The time had come to bid goodbye to Campeche town and state. We moved on into Yucatan, the land of the ancient Mayans.

Here, the houses were windowless, oval in shape with two open doorways opposite each other under a thatched roof. Each family had built their own house of bamboo, cemented together with mud and painted white. Each house, according to its owner's wealth, had some well-cultivated ground attached, which housed livestock and always palms. Each compound was surrounded by a rough stone wall. The churches were all Franciscan, built in their own style. The twin towers had disappeared instead they had what I call 'a sham front, extending above the roof'. Roads were mostly straight, running through flat land. We saw an arch built across the highway looming up in the distance. The ancient Mayans always built these at the entrance or exits of their towns. The Spaniards copied them and nowadays the arches mark the beginning of an ancient site. We were nearing one of the three important Mayan sites, the former Priest Town of Kabah.

We walked through the jungle. Although the trees here were often small, the undergrowth where it had not been cleared was often thick and dense. We had to watch our step, since there were treacherous holes, the 'Cenotes' or underground water holes. We climbed up the steps of the main pyramid in order to admire the facade of the temple, which was profusely decorated with many stylized Chaaks' heads. Close by stood the Temple of the Columns, with its overriding cornice which protected the walls, and with its now familiar crestella on top. We saw Chaak with a nose in the form of an elephant's trunk for the first time. Everywhere in Mayan culture, the mysterious 'X' met our eyes. This symbol has not been explained. It appeared in all kinds of guises, when we least expected it. Kabah, according to our guide, is pure Puuc architecture, dating back to about 100 BC. Evidence of an earlier civilisation had been found in Veracruz and Guatamala.

We saw our first iguana, sunning itself on the hot rock, as we were leaving this interesting site. We had but a short run before we reached our next destination: Uxmal. First, we cooled down in the pleasant hotel, built right in the middle of the jungle. Again, it was built in the style of an old hacienda, or perhaps it had served as such originally. Four sides enclosed a lush garden around a swimming pool, with most beautiful plants. Many orchids, alas not yet in bloom, grew on many trees.

The indigenous population of Yucatan are the descendants of the Mayans. The men are short and squat and the girls are rather plump. The girls' faces are clear and silky-skinned - they look happy and content. Their hair is thick and smooth, frequently adorned with a red bow at the back. They move slowly and gracefully, clad in their traditional dress: a white, straight cotton shift, elaborately embroidered around the square neck. The same border adorns the short sleeves and the uneven hem. This is called the Huipile worn over flounced skirts, which are trimmed with a broad border of handmade lace. They still adhere to their traditions and speak their own language.

We walked through the dense forest to gain the main road, crossed it and entered the famous site of Uxmal, pronounced 'Ushmal'. This means 'thrice built'. It was easily visible, that this had been done. The ancient Indians used to rebuild their temples and palaces after a set number of years. Uxmal was the city of the kings.

Directly inside the entrance loomed the dominant, oval structure of the House of the Wise Man. The oval-shaped houses of the Mayans are based on this pyramid. This pyramid was incredibly steep, crowned by two temples standing back to back, which could

House of the Wise Man (Uxmal).

Corbel Arch (Uxmal).

Chaak-Mol.

be reached by two separate staircases. An earlier temple had been discovered inside the pyramid. The style used in this edifice was called 'Chen' and was of pure Mayan origin.

We next entered the 'Nun's Quadrangle', a name chosen by archaeologists. The north building was the largest with steps leading to 88 rooms. The facade was richly ornamented with Chaaks and 'Xs' much in evidence. The elephant's trunks were differently curved than the ones we had seen in Kabah. This building, as in Kabah, was in pure 'Puuc' style. At either side of the staircase were altars with roofs supported by stout pillars. The east building had simple decorations and fewer rooms, but also built in 'Puuc' style. The west building had a good deal of decoration, which showed the influence of 'Toltec' side by side with pure 'Puuc'. It was the first time that the plumed serpent appeared. Here it was shown with the tail of a rattlesnake. There were human figures with the 'butterfly' covering their lower parts. Later, the butterfly was used as a breastplate. The famous phallic symbol was here, which was worshipped as a symbol of fertility. It was thought that the serpent was added much later, at the end of the Third Empire.

We walked through the Corbel Arch, looking up to the red hands on the ceiling. Some people believe that these were the imprint of the bloody hands of the slaves who built this arch. We came to the Ballcourt, which was under reconstruction. But even though it was incomplete, the basic plan was easy to perceive The high parallel walls bear the stone rings, jutting out into the air. Many broken stones, already numbered, lay neatly placed in a row, ready to be used. The wavy lines of the serpent were much in evidence. The game was a ritual one between two warring tribes. The ball was made of crude rubber and extremely hard. As in today's soccer, it could be touched by any part of the body, except by hand. The object was to put it through the stone ring, which was very small and obviously required a good deal of skill. The captain of the losing team was sacrificed to the gods, and all the property of his tribe was confiscated and his fellow tribesmen became slaves.

We climbed up a pyramid to reach a wide plateau. On top stood the Governor's Palace, a long, Puuc-styled building with a plain base and various doorways. It rested on a series of terraces. All decorations appeared in the upper frieze, running round the entire building. Glancing across the horizon we saw a curious structure on the skyline, known as the 'Dovecot', because of openwork decorations resembling nesting boxes of doves. On the same pyramid, apart from the Governor's Palace, stood the Temple of the Turtle. A square building with delightful turtles decorating the frieze. In the centre of the pyramid stood a big stone, half buried. No one knows its significance. Last, but by no means least, there was a square altar on the plateau with the famous double-headed jaguar upon it. The jaguars or tigers were worshipped and in almost every ancient place stands evidence of this. From time to time you find the double-headed jaguar with a slight depression between the heads. This is thought to have been a place of offering. Later we saw a Chaak-Mol, which has a human form and lies on his back, knees drawn up, the trunk providing the place to receive offerings. We saw this at Chichen-Itza. I hope the photographs will illustrate what I am trying to describe. It is extremely interesting to me that the whole mythology is so involved and men and beasts are so intertwined and interchanged at many stages.

    I ascended the steps to the top of the House of the Governor to admire the superb sculpture of the building. The view across was breathtakingly beautiful, with undulating lines of dark blue hills in the distance. Untold treasures must still lie buried below the platform on which we were standing. We looked across and saw yet another pyramid with the dilapidated Temple of the Witch on its pinnacle. It had not yet been restored.

    We left Uxmal reluctantly : it had been a superb site with a most enchanting hotel. I had woken early and had sat on the cool balcony outside our room, looking at the dense vegetation before me. Amongst this organised chaos stood two small huts. Local craftsmen produced their handicraft here, pottery and weaving. They even had a crude kiln. It had been very peaceful and pleasant after a very short shower of rain.

    We drove along the straight and dusty highway through poor and arid country, looking more like scrubland than anything else, on our way to Merida. Now and again we passed haciendas, conjuring up a past era of elegance and well being - for the few privileged at least. We drove through some villages and eventually stopped at Mune. We were immediately surrounded by children and young women, offering their embroidered blouses for sale. We bought some of these cool cotton ones and could not resist taking photographs of the women and children. This scene reminded us of Ethiopia, although these children were very shy and did not speak English.

We continued on to Merida, where we stopped in the Zocalo. This was a pleasant town, bustling with life. The square had most beautiful, big sybo and yew trees, expertly shaped, providing shade. The shoeshine boys were touting for customers and, as always, young lovers and old men were enjoying the sun. It was a particularly attractive square with the lovely Casa Montejo, which is now a museum. We ventured into the courtyard, which was surrounded by attractive, wide-arched colonnades; beamed ceilings lined the entrance hall. We wandered out into the sunny square again and admired the stuccoed facade of the Municipal Building, a row of small shops and eating places, housed beneath cool arches, and another official building. This one had a square, plain courtyard with murals on its walls. On the South side of the square stood the enormous cathedral, built in the colonial style.

We spent some time buying some of the special shirts, known as Guayaberas. We were pleased with our purchases. All streets in Merida were numbered, therefore it is quite easy to find one's bearings.

We drove through the now familiar landscape, here broken by the appearance of Sisal fields. These are cacti, which are specially cultivated and later cut in a particular fashion and partially processed by hand, before they reach the sisal factories. We reached the end of our journey and settled for our last night en route in yet another hotel, which stood at the dusty roadside, facing a trailer park used by Americans. Most of them were retired and had come en masse as a 'trailer cavalcade', thirty or more of them, to explore Mexico. We also saw a 'rolling hotel' from Germany. This was an enormous bus with an equally enormous trailer. The bus was used during the day, the trailer contained the sleeping quarters for forty people and a soup kitchen at the rear.

After a very scruffy buffet lunch, we set off for Chichen-Itza, our last site on this trip. Chi means 'mouth', Chen means 'well', and Itza is the name of the Mayan tribe who founded the city in 850 AD. We entered this site, which was very large and divided into three parts. North and south lie to either side of the highway and a third area of underground caves was found 8 km along the main road. We started north of the highway, glancing at The Castle looming up on our right. This enormous pyramid, which showed Toltec influence, is the only one made of rocks and was well preserved, only 25% had to be restored. It soared into the sky like a watch-tower. Warrior figures were carved on the door of the simple temple. Two staircases lead up to it. Archaeologists discovered that this was in fact a second pyramid. One of an older date is inside, but more of this monument later. We proceeded across the sun-drenched, parched ground along the old causeway, past the Temple of Venus. The sculpture here showed a human face inside the mouth of a snake. At an earlier age the Itza had venerated the plumed serpent. They called it Kukulkan, not Quetzalcoatl. Kukulkan symbolised the white man with the red beard, floating up to join the gods in Heaven and becoming the Morning Star. Somewhat incongruously, on top of the temple, dedicated to Venus, stood a helicopter. A Mexican company was making a film that day.

We walked along the stony path with small trees and thick undergrowth to either side, disturbing night birds into hasty flight. The ground was hard and dry and most forbidding, yet suddenly we found ourselves at the rim of a deep well. Here stood the key to why the Itzas chose this place to build their city. It explains the name. When they found the well, they knew that without rivers above ground, there were subterranean streams sufficiently large to supply water for them all. The Cenout we looked down on was their sacred well and many virgins had been offered to the gods in these cool waters. Many jewels set in gold and silver have been found at the muddy bottom of this well. We retraced our steps along the sunny causeway, admiring the many butterflies as we walked along. We passed a conical stone amidst the grass and our guide picked up another one to strike a note. This reminded us of the method used to strike a note outside the church in Asmara, where stones hang suspended, waiting to be struck.

We stood in front of the Temple of the Eagles and Tigers and admired the superb sculpture. The eagles were shown holding human hearts in their claws. They are a Toltec symbol, the jaguar is Mayan. Obviously at some time these tribes had joined up and fused their cultures. The Toltecs had their capital in Tula, near Mexico City, but forsook this and invaded Yucatan. They were warriors and called themselves Xiv, after their commander in Yucatan. They were the first tribe to establish a social strata. They separated the kings from the priests, and the warriors from the kings.

Behind the Temple of the Eagles and Tigers stood the Wall of Skulls. The dead were buried here after death, but after a set time their bones were exhumed and placed on a platform to be bleached by the sun. The skulls bore the names and ages of the deceased. The families used to come to pay homage to their dead. It was plain to see that this platform served to bear the skulls, since the whole of the wall was densely decorated with carved skulls. Almost next door to this sombre monument stood the ballcourt, which is the largest known and is well preserved. Both rings, through which the ball has to pass, have been reconstructed. Sculptures along the walls symbolise the games, confirming the religious connotations of this important ritual. Above the North end of the court towered the Temple of the Jaguar. Completely in Toltec style, it showed the conquest of the city by the Toltecs in a series of wall paintings with some of the colour still visible. This temple, originally a Mayan structure, was rebuilt by the Toltecs. Yet another Chaak-mol stood, protected by the temple roof, in proud isolation.

We spent some time on our own to visit the interior of the big pyramid of the castle. A few narrow steps took us in the first instance down before we climbed 68 well-worn steps to the top of the first pyramid. Before us stood two double jaguars, two chaak-mols. One beautifully carved and regal-looking in pink stone; the other most elaborately painted red with jade inlays for eyes, which glittered most lifelike when caught in a beam of light. Above these chaakmols were lovely stone carvings of rosettes and of more jaguars. We emerged again into brilliant sunshine, crossed the big plaza and felt the full impact of the group called The Thousand Columns surrounding the Temple of Warriors. This sea of broken columns was quite remarkable. They were square and solid. Many showed exquisite carvings on their four sides. We climbed up the steps of the pyramid to the temple. The walls here, once again, bore both Mayan and Toltec design. The roof had long fallen in, but in the centre of the temple stood a double row of snake columns. The bases of these forlorn columns consisted of serpents' heads, whilst their tails, freed now from all burdens, soar up into the sky. They used to support the roof. A well-preserved chaak-mol stood on the platform. Here again, it was possible to descend inside this pyramid to see the well-preserved parts of the former temple with carvings showing the conquest by the Toltecs. The colours, well protected from weathering, were in excellent condition. Before we climbed down from our lofty perch, we stood still to admire the view of this vast site.

We had little time before closing. We hurried off in search of the Caracol or Observatory, which stood south of the highway. This area was also known as Old Chichen-Itza. It was rarely shown to the tourists and has not been reconstructed. It was overgrown and appeals to me like a forgotten city, slumbering in the sun. We passed an enormous pyramid to our right, completely unrestored, and yet we could quite clearly perceive the majestic sweep of the grand staircase leading to the temple. Two huge, beautifully carved serpents' heads glared down on us from their lofty height. We hurried further on and came to a broad clearing in the jungle, the 'Plaza', surrounded by four temples. To the east of this fine square stood the remains of an unusual structure. A broad stairway led up to the round building called Caracol, which means 'snail' in Spanish and refers to the circular staircase inside. Unfortunately it was no longer safe to ascend and see the apertures in the walls of the domelike structure, which line up with certain stars on certain days, and were used by the priests to adjust the calendar and fix important dates for planting, reaping harvests, etc. We glanced across to the remains of some

Caracol (Chichen-Itza).

more buildings with some exquisite carvings. Alas, we were unable to linger, since time had come for this fascinating site to be closed for the night. We left reluctantly, passing some of the typical oval-shaped houses with their thatched roofs. One of them had the usual hammock slung across from beam to beam and a large refrigerator placed on the mud floor.

When we returned to our hotel, the electricity had failed. There was no air conditioning in our room, nor hot water in the tap, nor light. We sat by the pool, sipping a drink, and talked to some Americans, who had come from their caravans to take a dip in the pool. Later we dined by candle light until the power suddenly returned.

We strolled into the nearby village of Piste next morning . We wandered into a small artist's shop, but restrained ourselves from buying some of the attractive 'rubbings' of the sculptures done on bark. We left the dusty highway and walked along the stony tracks between the houses. They all stood in their own ground, no longer huddled close together. Wealth was judged by the size of the plot. By our standards, people were incredibly poor. To supplement their meagre existence, they planted palms and other fruit-bearing trees. A young woman with three children and a fourth on the way came out of her neat little house to greet us and was pleased for us to take photographs. No member of this little family looked very bright. We waved goodbye and looked at the cemetery with its garish coloured houses nearby.

We reached a bigger compound where the mother of the house was busily doing the washing. It appears that Sunday was wash-day in Piste. She asked us into the compound. We gathered that she was 38 years old and had ten children. The oldest daughter, who was assisting her, was in her twenties and, carrying a little toddler in her arms, was pregnant. One bright little boy drew water from the well. This family was obviously well to do. They had three little oval houses. The largest was the sleeping quarter, where they all slept in hammocks. These were neatly stowed away, slung across the beams during the day. All huts had mud floors, no windows, but two doorways opposite each other, to create a through draught, if possible. This family proudly displayed wardrobes and a dresser in their dormitory. The second, smaller hut provided their cooking and dining area, where they cooked on an open fire. The third and smallest of them all served as a pigsty. Chickens were scratching around and a couple of scraggy dogs were playing with the smaller children. We were permitted to photograph the children.

We left and turned to the highroad, which led us to the Zocalo, surrounded by shops, with the church in the centre. We entered through the churchwarden's living quarters and found two young girls busily chatting to each other, leisurely sweeping the floor of this simple church. Across the road stood a Presbyterian church, Eben-eezer by name, painted in a shocking green. A service was in progress and the little hall was well filled. Behind this hall, on an open terrace, a Sunday class was taking place. Alas, the youngsters paid more attention to us than to the blackboard.

We talked to a young man who was feeding his turkey outside his little house and who spoke fairly good English. He had learned it at school in Merida, in order to obtain a job in one of the hotels. He had three daughters, the oldest being ten years old. We wandered on and heard the strange sound of a machine. We traced it to one hut in which a simple grinding machine ground maize. Women and children came, carrying buckets and bowls of maize kernels on their heads and waited for it to be transformed into flour to carry back home again. We turned back towards our hotel but stopped once more, highly intrigued by the Tortilleria, where the ground floor was made into a dough by hand, flattened into little round pancakes, quickly baked, carefully counted and then handed to the respective customer. Uneven rounds were discarded. We tasted a sample of these rejects. They had no taste at all, being unleavened and therefore they require the sharpness of various fillings. Alternatively, it may be necessary to counterbalance the hot fillings with a bland foil. Whichever it was, the end result remained the same. The tortillas constitute the staple food of Mexico.

We said goodbye to Chichen-Itza and drove back along the road towards Merida, heading for the airport to bring us back to Mexico City. We stopped along the road to see a sisal factory, but it was closed, since it was Sunday. Lorries, with their loads of cut cacti piled high, stood outside the gates. Our guide went to a good deal of trouble to explain to us the processing of this produce and the versatility of this plant as used by the ingenious Indians in former days. They even used the spine with its sharp point, deftly extracting it, producing a needle with thread already attached. They were able to peel the outside thin cover and to compressed it into a type of papyrus.

We had enjoyed Yucatan and found it of great interest. We arrived in Mexico City in the evening after a short flight. Both airports, Merida and Mexico City were modern and very clean. Merida Airport was relatively empty, whereas Mexico City Airport was extremely busy.

Once again we settled down in the same hotel for our last few days in the city.

Next morning saw us on our way to Taxco or Tasco, the Silver City. We drove along the now familiar Reforma out of town, past many impressive monuments. The city, already the third largest in the world, is growing rapidly. There are satellite towns extending both sides of the highway and climbing up the lower sides of the surrounding hills. Square boxes after square boxes had been put up and looked quite soulless, surrounded by sun-baked soil. We passed cement works with a fortress-like building nearby, no doubt the private residence of one of the directors.

Once again we stopped at the toll gate to pay our due in order to reach the open road. The roads were excellent in Mexico and this one in particular was a superb scenic route, climbing up and down the mountains known as the Sierra Madres of Mexico, the geological continuation of the Rocky Mountains of Canada. Looking back from one particular point along this road, we had a beautiful view over the entire capital. The scenery was breathtakingly beautiful, with pinewoods either side, reminiscent of the Alps. We reached Guernavaca, capital of Morelos State. This is known as the 'City of Eternal Spring', because of its beautiful climate. It lies actually on top of a pyramid and is entirely surrounded by ravines. The ill-fated Maximillian and his Carlotta made Guernavaca one of their favourite residences. It is a very pleasant town. We drove through narrow little lanes, bustling with life, up to the Plaza de Congress. This was crowded with local inhabitants going about their business, with tourists like ourselves and the ever-present vendors.

It was sunny and mild with a feeling of utter relaxation and contentment in the air. We admired the Palacio de Cortes, now the seat of the Municipal Government. The enormous building seemed like a forbidding fortress and had been built at the brink of the deep ravine. Cortes, charmed by the mildness of the climate, chose Guernavaca as his place of residence. Incidentally, he introduced the sugar-cane into Mexico from Cuba and built the first sugar mill. We admired the white arched facade of the Palace of the Constitution before we left in search of the cathedral. We scurried down narrow cobbled lanes, up steep steps, over more cobblestones. The houses, which we hurriedly glimpsed in the side streets, were quite enchanting. It was easy to find the cathedral, since the massive dome was visible from the distance. It was an imposing building, which has been little changed since it was built, over four hundred years ago. As most churches in Mexico, it was built by Franciscan monks. Inside it was beautifully simple and well proportioned, with traces of murals on the walls. The altar was strangely modern, but its simple elegance went well with the serene atmosphere. We stepped out into the sun-drenched cloisters, which lay peacefully before us.

Almost adjacent to the cathedral stood another church with a baroque facade, but quite plain inside. We crossed the garden and stood in amazement outside the Capilla de la Tercera Order de San Francisco, in the southwest corner of the cathedral precinct. This was a most remarkable building. The intricate decorations of its facade were lovingly worked by Indian sculptors, who covered the wall with artlessly carved plants and animals. The interior was dazzling with its profusion of ornate sculpture covered by gold leaf. There was yet another small chapel opposite the Capilla, less ornate. The whole complex was surrounded by a thick wall, resembling a formidable fortress.

Unfortunately we had no time to visit the famous Borda Gardens close by. Jose La Borda, or Jose de la Borda, was a Frenchman, who came to Mexico in 1716. He fell on bad times and

Cathedral of Guernavaca.

saddled his mule to make for Mexico City to seek his fortune. On his way across the mountains his mule stumbled and fell. Bending down to help his trusted steed to regain its legs again, he found a silver vein. This brought him immense fortune. In his gratitude he later built Santo Prisco in Tasco, saying, 'God gives to Borda: Borda gives to God'. He settled in Guernavaca; his son laid out the famous gardens in Tasco, known by his name.

We quickly bought a hammock and another big basket on the busy sunny square, before continuing our journey. Very soon we left the wooded scenery behind and found ourselves once more in the tropics. There were many varied shades of the pretty jacaranda tree; acacias with brown seedpods and many more different trees grew here. One bore cotton-wool-like flowers, which were a favourite source of nectar for the bees. Beehives were very much in evidence. We saw rice paddies, now dry and barren, for the first time. The rainy season starts in June and by the end of August all is fresh after the torrential rain. There were many cacti at both sides of the road. We stopped suddenly, forewarned by our guide that he would show us iguanas. These are eaten as specialities - fried, I think. They provide some much-needed protein. Apparently, Mexicans also collect worms, whose habitat is the centre of a certain cactus. These they also fry and eat to add protein to their diet. The scene which confronted us was cruel and crude: children, some barely toddlers, and a few women in rags, dragged the iguanas along the ground by a piece of string or carried them on their heads, or let them climb all over their bodies. It reminded me of the jewel-studded bugs on chains which we had seen in a shop window in Veracruz. Later a Canadian tourist had shown us these wretched insects confined in a special wooden box. To my utter horror, I learnt that they were worn as brooches by the fashionable women of Vancouver. They needed no water and lived on chips of wood.

The road began to climb and, after a series of bends, we arrived at Tasco, a charming little town which has been declared a National Monument. The picturesque houses climb up the wooded mountainside with their red tiled roofs glowing warmly in the sun. It was a pleasant sight, gladdening our hearts after the scene with the iguanas. We stopped at the lower part of town. A well-known ploy, ostensibly to 'have a rest and a drink' in one of the many silver shops. After a most indifferent meal, we were dispatched by taxis to the town proper, which lies poised on the mountainside, with twisting, narrow, cobbled lanes. Quite impossible for buses to negotiate the steep gradient up to the town or cope with the narrow lanes.

We spent a wonderful day in this delightful town. Every step proved pure enchantment. We browsed amongst the silver shops and, throwing all caution to the wind, bought six beautiful platters, silver plated on nickel. These were used all over Mexico as table-mats.

Well pleased with our purchase, we strolled along to the delightful Cathedral Square, dominated by the pink stone church of Santa Prisca. Its dome is decorated with brightly coloured glazed tiles, which we had seen shimmering in the distance on our approach to Tasco. The facade was richly decorated in pure baroque. Around the square were lovely houses of colonial architecture. The ground floors were now used as silver shops, whilst the floors above served as hotels and restaurants. Almost next to the cathedral stood the Casa la Borda, which had two stories facing the square, but four on the other side, facing the steep mountain slope. We found another, most elaborate house, the Casa Figuera, which is now used as a picture gallery. We looked for the William Sprengle Museum of Local Culture, but found it closed.

I left my friend and wandered off on my own., catching glimpses now and again of shady courtyards and walking past local schools with children wearing traditional uniforms. I popped into the very old and simple little church of Veracruz. Retracing my footsteps through yet another steep and cobble-stoned lane, I found Casa Humboldt, where the well known German naturalist lived for many years. This too was used as a shop, with lovely articles of exquisite craftsmanship reminiscent of Kashmiri ware. I stepped inside this cool Aladdin's cave and wandered out again into the sun-drenched courtyard. Rejoining my friends in the plaza, we went into the cathedral. Once again we found the full impact of the heavily ornate, gold-encrusted carving almost too much to bear. In the chapter-house were portraits of past worthies of the community by

Atlantas (Tula).

one of Mexico's famous painters of the 18th century, Miguel Cabera. Before finally leaving this enchanted city, we found a small silver shop where the artist designed and worked each exquisite article himself. We bought a silver Star of David on a heavy chain for Ruth, to replace one which we had purchased in Jerusalem and which had been stolen in a burglary.

Well satisfied with our day we returned to Mexico City. Darkness fell and, coming down the excellent road, we suddenly saw the whole of Mexico City beautifully illuminated under the dark sky.

Refreshed after our night's sleep we set off once more next day. This time we travelled northwest of the city. We were a small party, the three of us, a young Japanese couple with a two-year-old little girl and a brash Austrian, dressed up 'a la Mexican'.

Our road took us through the industrial section of the town. Soon we were in absolute desert, or so it seemed. Flat, dry and arid land surrounded us. There was little vegetation and at first it appeared very sparsely populated. The skyline in the distance was impressive, with many mountain chains, with strangely shaped peaks. Some looked truly volcanic cones, others were probably ancient pyramids, still undisturbed, slumbering beneath the soil. Nearing our destination, Tula, the former capital of the Toltecs, we passed oil refineries. Nearby stood many boxlike houses clustered together, provided for the workers of the refineries. At last Tula appeared in front of us, with the enormous statues of the Atlantas towering into the sky. As always, nearby were the gaunt ruins of a long-forgotten monastery of Cortes' time.

It was a bitterly cold day, with the wind sweeping cruelly across the vast site. All ancient towns were built high up on hills to be able to detect any approaching enemy. We first visited the tiny museum with some lovely original sculptures and other treasures found on the site. It was a most impressive place. The Toltecs - no one is certain whence they arrived - were master-builders, of that there is no doubt. They built pyramids from adobe - sunbaked mudbricks - which were remarkably well preserved. These were then faced with well-dressed stone and usually whitewashed. We saw sculptures still bearing the original colours: red for life, blue for water, green for agriculture and yellow for the wind. The Toltecs obviously worshipped the elements and nature, performing ceremonial dances in honour of their gods on an open air stage in the large square surrounding the altar.

The walls of their temples were most elaborately adorned. Their favourite theme was the feathered serpent, the symbol of their principal deity Quetzacoatl. There was a complete wall of serpents forming part of the temple devoted to this god. Here we saw for the first time the Greek Key motif as part of the decorative scheme. We found a most lovely Chaak-mol again, turning its head to look towards the West. The jaguar was again much in evidence as we walked around the site. There was a court of many columns with numerous altars, but we only found one reservoir to catch the precious rainwater. This reservoir appeared to be pitifully small for such a vast complex. According to my information, it was because of drought and internal strife that the Toltecs forsook Tula and wandered off to reappear in Yucatan and other parts of Mexico and America. We glanced at the ballcourt, which was the oldest that had been discovered. Last, but by no means least, we climbed the steep and well-worn steps of Quetzalcoatl's Pyramid to get a first-hand view of the 'Atlantas', giant columns, some round, others square, supporting the roof of the temple. They had been placed on top of the pyramid so that passing travellers could see them from far afield and would come close to inspect this most important site. I was intrigued to find that once again the 'peg and hole' method had been used to lock the massive blocks of stone together to form these enormous columns. They were richly carved and support the exquisitely sculptured heads.

As it was bitterly cold, we did not linger, but proceeded to our next port of call, the reconstructed village of Tepotzotla with its reconstructed monastery. We drove past the oil refineries, through arid land, back to the beginning of the industrial development. Part of this was still being built. Roads were already climbing up the slopes, electricity had been already laid on. Factories and houses had not been started to be erected. We left the busy highway which leads back to Mexico City and suddenly found ourselves jogging along cobbled streets into a delightful square, dominated by the old Jesuit Seminar of San Martin. This consisted of a whole complex of churches, chapels and patios, all built in colonial style.

Before continuing our sightseeing, we called a halt to partake of a welcome tequila and toasted sandwich to warm and sustain our chilled bodies. Fortified we stepped out into the square again. The main church, pure baroque, had a very highly decorated facade with only one single, lofty tower, which was curiously placed to the right side of the imposing entrance. We did not see the interior of this particular church, but walked along the shady path to enter the thick-walled church of St. Xavier. The wealth and impact of the exuberantly decorated churrigeresque altars were quite dazzling. We walked past the replica of a house of a nobleman of the 18th century. It stood within the walls of the complex between the church of St. Xavier and a small chapel. The house, partly tiled and complete in every detail, had its own small altar. We entered the little chapel behind the house, which was covered in gold. Its crowning glory was the dome, which was not exactly round, but built in tiers and highly ornamented with carved statues of the four archangels. The whole dome was caught in perfect reflection in a mirror, cleverly placed on the marble floor beneath. On our way out of this building we noticed the opaque window in one of the side chapels, made from onyx.

We paid a short visit to one of the patios surrounded by cloisters. This contained two cisterns, which were under repair.

We continued our journey to a small, strange village, called Tenayuca, at the foot of Cerro Tonoyo. which means the 'Walled City'. Tenayuca was founded by Xolote, King of the Chimec tribe, who had dwelt here since time immemorial. A very attractive, plain statue of King Xolote stood on the pleasant green. To the right of the green rose a Spanish church, to the left the most amazing Aztec pyramid, which dates back to the 13th century. As almost everywhere along the trail we followed in and around Mexico City, here too, the mighty Aztecs had conquered earlier tribes. The pyramid stood in the middle of the long-forgotten village, surrounded on three sides by cobbled streets. The fourth faced the green and the statue of proud King Xolote. The houses of the village were all enclosed by thick walls, as if to carry on the old tradition of the 'Walled City'.

The Aztecs added a new part to each pyramid after a set number of years. The pyramid of Tenayuca had eight eras, but only seven remained. The sloping walls were interrupted by platforms. On the west side was a double staircase with a central ramp. The whole structure was extremely impressive in its stark simplicity. Around the base, on three sides of the pyramid, were crudely modelled serpents' heads, some large, others small. According to our guide the size reflected the good fortune or the bad of a particular year. This pyramid had been covered by the Indians themselves and had never been detected by the Spaniards. Therefore it was well preserved and had not been mutilated.

We had hoped to continue on to visit yet another pyramid, called Santa Cecilia, just five kilometres further along the road. We were, however, frozen stiff and glad to return to Mexico City once again.

Back in town, having rested for some time, Ruth and I set forth to buy shoes for myself. In the first shop, the young man who served us left us standing to chat to a friend. We walked out. The next shop looked as if it were closed for the night. The girls were engaged in leisurely sweeping and washing the floor. We gingerly asked whether it was closing time. But no, the shop remained open for business until 8pm; it had just gone 6pm. The young lady, who bestirred herself in the usual languid fashion to serve us, served us well. Although her demeanour remained unchanged, she actually took endless trouble to find a pair of shoes to fit my difficult feet.

Our last day in Mexico dawned. As if to get us acclimatised to the weather back home in England, it was grey and cold. A true November day.

We had arranged to meet Isobel again. She had suggested taking us to a glass factory and a market in town. We had not made any further plans, depending entirely on what our kind hostess had in mind. As it turned out, we spent the whole day in her company and had a marvellous time in spite of the grey, overcast skies and steady rain at the end of the day. It never rains in Mexico until June, we were assured, but this year bad weather had swept into Mexico from America. It snowed in Houston, Texas, which was not far away.

We drove through the Reforma and eventually ended up in a poor quarter of the town. Isobel manoeuvered her big car expertly and parked at the kerbside, fully aware that one of the pathetic creatures on the pavement would act as self-appointed attendant to the car. Life was beginning to stir. The Indians were setting out their different wares on the pavement. We followed our guide, who took us swiftly through a narrow street, the Covent Garden of Mexico City, so it appeared. I have never seen such mountains of gigantic, juicy pineapples, eighteen pence for two. There were big depots of oranges and grapefruits, enormous tomatoes and other fruit. We stopped at a very old building which was a glass factory and stepped into the courtyard. Here the processing began. Old bottles were sorted according to their colours. Their tops were knocked off, their labels removed, they were crudely smashed and ready for the smelting pot. The factory was one large, lofty building with one big smelting furnace and many ovens for baking and subsequent cooling of the newly fashioned articles. We watched the perfect team-work in utter fascination. A dozen men or so were making wineglasses, some small, others large, all blown by mouth and deftly turned and trimmed by hand. We each were presented with a glass flower. We went into the showroom, where shelf upon shelf displayed neatly arranged glassware. Each section in its different colour. We felt, of course, obliged to buy but are well pleased with our choice. We crossed the courtyard once more to visit the small 'museum'. This enterprise was a family business, founded a hundred years ago by two brothers and now continued by the third generation. The museum contained some show-cases, one with tropical flowers, another with tropical fauna, two others displayed biblical scenes. All this had been made by the founders and, if lost, could not be replaced. In one corner of the room was a small leather factory and its proprietor acted as self-appointed custodian of the museum. He was a talkative, kindly Jew, who we felt certain hailed from eastern parts of Central Europe. We bought a small bag we had been looking for, convenient for holding a passport, and parted the best of friends.

Time had come to collect young Sally and her Mexican friend

from play-school. Once again we negotiated the Reforma, drove through Chapultepec Park up to the lofty heights of the elegant residential quarter. We deposited Sally's friend at his front gate and turned once more towards the centre of town. This time to yet a different quarter to see the pottery market. Again, Isobel did not seem to hesitate about where to park the car. It was a one-armed man, looking for all the world like a pirate, who guarded the car.

Markets never fail to fascinate me. this one was a most amazing microcosm. We entered by the backdoor, so to speak, past the garbage heap next to a restaurant. Part of the market had been given over to pottery. Anything from gigantic cauldrons down to minute dolls, mugs and plates, were for sale. Everything was displayed in large quantities, all was hand-made, down to the last detail, and each article was painted with appropriate patterns. There were tiny brooms and brushes too, wooden kitchen utensils and other things. Some stalls sold articles made from reconditioned tins, such as funnels, strainers, watering cans, lamps, etc. These reminded us of Ethiopia and Ladakh.

We walked up and down the aisles in total bewilderment at the profusion of goods. Heaven only knows who bought all this multitude offered for sale. The next part of the market was equally absorbing, consisting of a large number of medical stalls, offering all kinds of herbs for every conceivable ailment which might befall body or mind. Some stalls had religious items for sale, such as incense, joss sticks and mystic potions. Last, but not least, there was a section of livestock. Hens with their little chicks, ducks with their ducklings, turkeys side by side with rabbits and pigeons. There were large numbers of birds in tiny cages. Some we knew, such as canaries, budgerigars, parrots and parakeets, but many of them we could not name - tiny chaps with lovely, bright colours. The poor chickens were tied together in pairs.

Isobel, much to little Sally's delight, bought a white Mrs. Rabbit for Lucy. Lucy already had Snowy, a white male, but he had lost his mate. The poor small creature Isobel bought looked a trifle moth eaten, I must confess. Lucy was slightly disappointed at first. However, I assured her that, given good care and attention, her little pet would blossom forth and become a most beautiful rabbit with silky, shiny fur.

Once again we passed the spices, many unfamiliar to us. I think the poor people utilised everything Nature provides. They even infused woodchippings. We passed the garbage heap again and watched poor women raking amongst the rubbish to rescue green leaves, discarded by their peers. Isobel thanked the one-armed bandit and paid him well-earned pesos for guarding the car. We now returned once more to town, complete with Mrs. Rabbit, to call on Francis in his office.

We tried in vain on our way to cash some English travellers cheques in one of the many banks. Only one bank in town dealt with sterling. However, Francis came to our rescue and cashed a cheque for us. His office was in the British-Mexican Institute, an attractive, modern building, at present however under alterations, and fine dust formed a film over everything. This did not detract from the hospitality offered. We all crowded into Francis' little office for light refreshments. A large cardboard box was found for the latest acquisition, which had been gently carried in a plastic bag till then. She shared our lunch hour quite happily in Francis' wastepaper basket.

We bade farewell to our host and once more joined the incredible throng of traffic, heading this time towards the University, looking for the archaeological site of Copilco. I had read about this in one of our guidebooks and thought it sounded quite intriguing. We turned off the broad, busy avenue and found ourselves suddenly in a little oasis of cobbled streets, surrounding an area of grass. Attractive stone arches spanned the little green. There were imposing buildings to one side of the triangular space and a modern residential quarter stood adjacent to them. We had great difficulties in finding our goal. We drove through poor streets at the other side of the triangle, thronged with children, dogs and old people. Old and young alike were laughing happily and joking. Two old men directed us, one stating that our journey would be of no avail, the second eagerly encouraging us to try. We found the site and both old men were right. It was officially closed, but once again, a word from Isobel and gates opened for us. We found a warren of tunnels below an enormous lava rock . We looked into the mouth of one of them and saw the original paving stones. Skeletons, which were identified as belonging to an anthropological type close to modern man, have been discovered here. All articles found here have been removed to the Museum of Anthropology and have been cleverly displayed in a mock-up lava cave in the grounds. Isobel thanked our kind 'curator', but he refused the proffered reward.

We returned to the highway. Driving past the imposing Olympic Stadium with its enormous mosaic, we entered the University 'City'. We drove through lovely woods out into the complex of large buildings set amongst green grass. The most outstanding building was the library, with a mural by Juan O'Gorman (not of Irish origin). It was indeed impressive, since all colours were achieved using natural stones.

As we returned to the car, it started to rain. We made a short stop to see the beautiful flower market with daffodils, tulips, pansies and chrysanthemums as well as roses, carnations, bird of paradise flowers and other exotic blooms. The arrangements were mostly in baskets and slender vases and looked very artistic. Adjoining the market was a craft shop specialising in carpets based on the Persian technique. In passing, we noticed an imposing building next to the craft shop. It must have been a monastery once upon a time, but now served as Regional Museum. Mexico City boasts of many fine museums, but our time was too short to explore them all.

To complete the day, Isobel drove us to a different district of the city, the quarter called Los Angeles. She showed us one more plaza, tranquil with its cobbled pavements, where artists showed their pictures and sculptures at the weekend. On an adjacent square, the Indians from the surrounding villages pitched their tents and erected little huts each Saturday to sell their wares. Unfortunately we never were able to see an Indian market.

Our last stop was in Los Angeles to visit one of the former private casas, now open to the public, in order to see the domestic architecture and furniture. In the courtyard - all colonial buildings surround a courtyard - was a fountain. This was decorated with ceramic plates and cups and jugs, with oyster shells and looked unusual and colourful. The rooms were furnished with heavily carved chairs, tables and chests, and hung with lovely mid-European paintings.

Isobel took us back to her home to see the children, before we parted. A welcome cup of tea refreshed us all. We drove once more down the Reforma, this time in pouring rain. We returned to our hotel to dine, to pack our belongings, to sleep for the last time in Mexico. It rained all night, but stopped by the morning.

We went for a last time for a walk in Alameda Park, before it was time to board our bus. This time we drove through the back streets, past old and sadly decrepit houses, to reach the airport. Haze hovered over Mexico City as our plane rose into the sky. Soon we climbed above the clouds into sunshine. We flew across Miami Beach and looked down on the golden sands and tall square buildings, reaching for the sky. The sea was blue and now and then little boats were easily discernible. Further along we saw a large steamer gliding along majestically.

We called again at Freeport. Blue sea lapped around the shores of the island. Tall, lovely trees stood sentry over the flat land. The wooded parts were neatly intersected by straight roads. In other parts, equally straight artificial waterways ran through sandy soil. A stately mansion queened it over a vast estate with many golf courses easily seen from the air. We took off again after a short while and a chain of tiny islands appeared below us. Soon evening fell and the bright blue sea turned to inky black. A band of deep pink faded into a pale peach before it was swallowed up by the dark sky. I liked the dramatic sunset over the ocean.

We landed at Bermuda. Once again, wind, rain and cold greeted us. We were informed that the plane had developed engine trouble and were asked to disembark. We waited patiently in the uninspiring transit lounge. Secretly we had hoped for a delay, to have a short reprieve and see Bermuda. But it was not to be. After just one hour's wait, we were airborne once more.

The rest of our journey was rather turbulent, but entirely uneventful. We touched down in time. Our luggage was buried below the freight. It therefore took some time to retrieve our cases and then to wait for the airport bus. A learner driver took us round the houses back to Victoria Air Terminal. It was the end of one more fascinating journey.

P.S. Sadly, Francis and Isobel's marriage did break up. We saw the family twice again, both times in Delhi. We did not meet when they were back in England, quite near to us. They divorced in 1993.

Lima
19 March 1979

We have arrived after what appeared to be a very long journey, but time is a strange concept. London, New York, the journey itself, have already receded, both in time and space.

We arrived very early at London Airport, having been given a lift by a couple who are in our party. There was little traffic on the road to the airport, but London Airport was full to the brim. We were two hours late, leaving in an enormous jumbo jet. The time went very quickly. It is always interesting to watch other people around you - all shapes, all sizes, all colours, all races. I am generally quite happy as long as I can bury my nose in a book. I was able to do just that, trying to read about the ancient civilisation of Peru.

Finally we took off and actually made up time with a strong tailwind behind us. Even the sun had come out over London to bid us goodbye. We flew over the English countryside, covered by snow, before heading out over the Atlantic.

We had a pleasant fellow traveller, an Englishman, who had emigrated to Baltimore twelve years ago. He was a doctor, trained at Charing Cross Hospital, married to a nurse. They had four daughters. He specialised in plastic surgery and had become interested in ancient medical instruments and showed us a beautifully illustrated book which he had just bought.

We crossed the snow-covered countryside of Newfoundland and soon approached Kennedy Airport, where we disembarked. There was a certain amount of confusion concerning our luggage, but even that was fairly soon sorted out and we were free to leave. My niece Hilari was waiting for us right in front of all the crowd, having sent her husband and Michelle, their adopted little girl, for a walk. Ruth, my friend and travel companion, met her classmate of 41 years ago and his Dutch wife. We left the airport, which is huge. Each airline has its own building.

The first sight of the USA struck us like driving through a frontier town once we had left the highway and were following sandy roads. Small houses in gay colours, some clad in wood, lined the roadside. We were taken to a comfortable restaurant where we could sit over a meal and talk to our hearts' content. We said goodbye to Ruth's friends and returned to the airport to spend the remaining time chatting to Hilari and Jim, and getting acquainted with young Michelle, who was obviously excited at meeting her two new aunts, but appeared remarkably relaxed and happy with her newly found parents. Americans seemed friendly and many chatted with the little girl and all of them smiled at her. It was soon time to say goodbye and check in at the Peruvian Airline.

It was absolute shambles trying to pay the airport tax and get the seats allotted to us. Eventually we were settled in the more spacious Trident to continue our flight. Once again we were late in taking off. We flew all night. At first there was room to stretch out, until Miami, where we filled up. I went for a walk around Miami's elegant airport, just to have a change. Food was served at regular intervals, nicely presented, light and adequate. We slept, we read and watched a film at 3 am. I watched the sun rise over the ocean, suddenly a new day had begun. At last we landed at Lima, where we met our fellow travellers and our leader.

Formalities completed, we boarded a waiting coach and drove into town. Like so many other towns, Lima is surrounded by shanty towns. Some buildings had not been completed, others had already fallen into disrepair. We crossed the gorge of the river Rima, where shacks clung precariously to the sides. We neared the centre and caught glimpses of some magnificent colonial houses, particularly around the main square, The Plaza de Armas, the heart of the city. A spacious square, it is well laid out with a bronze fountain playing in its centre. It is surrounded by important buildings, all remarkably new, but still built in the colonial style: the large cathedral linked to the lovely Bishop's Palace and the Governor's Palace, where the guards in white breeches and red coats with glittering helmets stand outside the enormous iron gate to protect it. Many of these buildings have attractive wooden closed-in balconies, a feature of Peru. They are often beautifully carved with lattice windows. They date back to Moorish times in Spain, when women were hidden away. Thus the ladies of the house could watch life outside in the streets from their wooden balconies without being seen.

Luckily our small hostel stood only a stone's throw from the Plaza de Armas. After a short rest, we sallied forth to explore. It was easy to find our way to the Plaza de Armas and from there to the shopping street, Jiron de la Union. Being Sunday, the shops were closed, but people in their Sunday best were promenading. We noticed the finely carved facade of the church La Merced. We continued our leisurely walk to another square, Plaza San Martin, with a statue of the South American hero Simón Bolívar proudly displayed on his horse. We wandered down a broad avenue, highly intrigued by the many street vendors displaying their splendid wares on the ground. Many artists exhibited their paintings of streets in Lima and of mountain scenes. Many of the latter showed the llama. We continued, making our way to yet another square, Plaza de Grau, past the very impressive Palace de Justice, the Peruvian Law Courts. Once again there was an imposing monument in the centre of the plaza - that of de Grau, obviously a naval man, with an anchor and a sailor standing guard. I learned at a later stage that De Grau was a famous Peruvian admiral.

The Peruvians appear to be incredibly fond of monuments and statues. Outside the Palace de Justice are attractive bronze animals: a group of nine llamas, a roaring lion, a puma and a team of water-buffalos led by an Indian. Families were out and lifted children up to ride on the bronze animals. We took a photograph of two little ones on the back of the puma.

We were actually on our way to the Museum of Art. We passed the charming little Museum of Italian Art, standing in a pretty little park, before reaching our destination. This too was a handsome building. It housed a splendid collection of Peruvian culture from the 2,000-year old Paracas civilisation up to the present time. We concentrated on the pre-Inca times and enjoyed looking at the ceramics and the well-preserved textiles. All these artifacts had been found in tombs. No written record exists. Curiously, script was unknown, even to the advanced Incas; therefore most knowledge is derived from the dead. They were buried in their tombs swathed in cloth, accompanied by ceramic vessels and statues. Most burial chambers have been looted many moons ago and all that remains are mummy bundles and pottery.

We quickly glanced at the ornate articles from the times of the Conquistadores. The furniture was heavily carved, frequently skilfully inlaid with mother of pearl and silver. The paintings were of religious subjects, mounted in elaborate silver frames. Some of the modern paintings were most attractive, but we had no time to linger. Well pleased with ourselves, we slowly walked back to our hotel, taking a different avenue back to the Plaza de Armas. Many of the houses we passed were sadly dilapidated, exposing the structure behind the plaster, which consisted of wooden poles slung together to resist earthquakes. The last extensive earthquake struck Lima in 1970, causing untold damage.

We noticed that the Peruvians, in spite of the humid heat, like physical contact, like the Mexicans. A good deal of quite uninhibited petting goes on in all the parks, contrary to one's expectations of a Catholic society.

We met up with the rest of our party to listen to an introductory talk by our tour leader. The atmosphere seemed very informal; the trip promised to be extremely interesting.

We were fortunate to have a bedroom facing out on the complex of church and monastery of San Francisco. Life went on from early morning right through the night, when we could hear voices drift up. Some people sat on the seat in the square, conversing in the middle of the night, whilst others, poor souls, wrapped up in thin rags, settled in the various porches of the church for their night's rest. Morning dawned, and suddenly out of nowhere vendors appeared, setting up their stalls. The first customers arrived on the scene and started to make their purchases. Always, on every square, as in Mexico, the photographer was in evidence, taking up his position early in the morning and arranging his old-fashioned plate camera. People came and people went. But women, so familiar in Spain in their black dresses, were entirely absent in Peru.

The sun was hot and soon the bare hills behind the city were hidden by heat haze. Later I learned that this was not heat haze, but pollution. Fruit stalls, offering a great variety, arrived on the scene. Customers chose their own fruit. Peaches were carefully brushed, before being finally sold. Stalls selling crushed icecubes topped with fruit syrup had joined the others and soon cook stalls, frying meat and other tit-bits, had been set up. Later, when the day drew to a close, more restaurant stalls appeared, which were very much frequented. There were also many eating places around the square, some clean, others more dubious. Small boys with plain wooden boxes tried hard to persuade people to have their shoes cleaned. They were the only ones to have noticed the strangers in their midst. There were only very few tourists besides ourselves in Lima. We met a few youngsters, who were seeing the country on a shoestring budget, eating in simple bars and sleeping in primitive hotels.

We started our second day in the city with a tour of the town. Unfortunately, neither the driver of our coach nor the local guide were very helpful, since the first did not know his way and the second had a very poor command of English, in spite of the fact that he had lived in America for four years and also seemed to have little knowledge of the town. Fortunately our tour leader filled in the gaps.

We saw the treasures of the Church of Fan Francisco, which were most impressive, consisting of silver candlesticks and silver chalices, heavily embroidered vestments of gold, silver and precious stones, of paintings and statues. Our tour leader begged us to forget the true British inhibition and rejection of the opulent style of the Conquistadores, which of course is pure baroque and alien, generally speaking, to English taste. The cloisters, as all cloisters do, formed a serene oasis surrounding cool gardens full of lush semi-tropical plants. Bulls-eye round windows pierced the upper galleries of the surrounding buildings.

Our next port of call was the Plaza de Armas, where we stepped inside the cool cathedral, which has some lovely wooden carved altars and choir stalls of plain wood, not gilded as in Mexico. Strangely, neither candles nor incense were used in the churches in Peru. In a small chapel stood a glass coffin with Pizarro's shrivelled remains. Their authenticity has been questioned in recent times.

We were taken to the Museum of the Inquisition. Apart from

the Senate Room, with a beautifully carved ceiling, we would have happily omitted this grisly visit. To see the contrast between the shanty town, which had greeted us on our arrival and the elegant colonial style, which we had observed that morning, with the decay of many buildings blatantly in evidence amongst the splendour, was truly amazing. To counterbalance this, we were taken to the sophisticated suburb of Miraflores with broad tree-lined avenues and attractive villas set in lovely gardens with a profusion of luxurious plants. We stopped for a quick snack before driving to the beach for a dip in the ocean. The rollers were terrifying and swept most of us off our feet. One little old lady injured her knee. This was the fourth mishap which had struck the party. On our arrival one Welsh lady had lost her case on the journey. Another had had her wrist-watch snatched from her arm, and on the following day one of the ladies had developed shingles. In spite of all this, no one seemed unduly disturbed, nor distressed enough to spoil the atmosphere of relaxed pleasure.

 I set off later on my own to find San Pedro, one of the many beautiful churches in Lima. A service was in progress, but nobody took any notice of me listening to the beautiful organ playing, and admiring the superb woodcarvings.

 My next quest was to find the Torre Tagle Palace, the city's best surviving specimen of colonial architecture. It was quite exquisite, with its wooden carvings, its balcony and pebbled courtyard. By then it was dark and the streets had been taken over by street vendors displaying their wares on the ground. The town was teeming with people. I discovered a beautiful bookshop with a number of excellent books in English. Unfortunately we were not able to find time to return to buy, which I regretted, since one of the books I coveted is out of print in England.

 I stopped to look at the church La Merced. Again, the evening service had begun and added warmth and dignity to the beauty of this church and in particular the fine voices of the choirboys.

 That night we dined out at another hotel which was in an utter shambles, and we were not surprised to learn later that it was closing down because of lack of business. Whatever we ordered did not appear, and half an hour later we were informed that the food we had ordered was 'off', but no one grumbled.

We packed next morning, leaving our main luggage behind at the hotel, ready for our departure to Trujillo later in the day. We drove to the Museum of Anthropology and Archaeology, which was meant to open at 8.30 am, but someone had changed his or her mind and delayed the opening hour until 10 o'clock. We used the time in hand to see Simón Bolívar's Museum, his Residence, which formed part of the museum complex.

It was interesting to learn a little history and hear about the man who meant so well, but ultimately achieved so little. Altogether, the present state of the Indians is very sad. After reaching great heights, they have descended to second-class citizens and are still being exploited. There is no freedom for them yet. We did not really understand the situation, since it has been a long time since the Spanish yoke had been broken. We spent the rest of the morning in the main museum. Our tour leader excelled himself: his lucid comments were much appreciated. We walked past the prehistoric exhibits, and started with the Chavin culture. These people lived in the Sierra in the centre of the Andes, from approximately 900 - 200 BC. They were interested in textures. Their designs were stylized with felines, eagles and hawks in evidence, strongly reminiscent of the Olmec culture in Mexico, with its jaguar design. Chavin pottery was stone-like in texture, with heavy patterns in relief. The pots had characteristic stirrup spouts. The later Chavin pots were red in colour. We saw the intricate Raimondi Stelae depicting the Staff God. The staff symbolises thunderbolts, akin to those of Zeus and Thor.

Another culture, overlapping partly with the mountain culture of Chavin, was Kotosh, which existed on the coast and defied the accepted concept that settled tribes need agriculture. They did not practice agriculture, but lived off the sea and rivers, which had an abundance of fish.

We looked at exhibits of other cultures, which at existed roughly the same time in various parts of Peru. Paracas culture from 200 BC to the birth of Christ, Nazca from the birth of Christ to 600 AD, and Salimu, Chimu and Mochian cultures. Chimu pottery had typical shapes with whistling jars. The sound of these played an important part in their religious ceremonies. These pots were grave offerings, hence they are so well preserved. Gourds and pan pipes were also used. All these artifacts were connected with the after-life. Puscara culture, approximately from 200 BC, was a subsidiary culture, based between the much later Inca capital of Cusco and Lake Titicaca. This has not as yet been explored. Paracas was a desert culture, represented by the most impressive Tello Obelisk, which is difficult to interpret. It is meant to represent a lizard. Paracas culture still retained the fine elements. Tusks were easily distinguished, eyes became more normal, the Bell element emerged. There was a continuation of infinity. It was quite fascinating, once one had grasped this concept, to follow it through in their ceramics and textiles. Their pots were painted before being baked. They showed characteristic bridge spouts. The Paracas existed in the South, simultaneously with the Mochians in the North, roughly from the birth of Christ to 800 AD. Nascan followed on Paracas and Chavin, still using the tongue-into-head-and-tongue phenomenon. Their pottery was painted after firing. Nascan progressed to more abstract designs and was divided into eight epoches. It was a river/valley culture, depicting birds, beasts and flowers in its ceramics, before they became abstract.

The Moche ceramics were divided into five different epoches, according to the style of their spouts. There were four to five heights of pottery. The colours were red and white. Portrait jars appeared. These looked wonderfully alive. Their male god was the Sky God, sitting in the lotus position on a mountainside, staring into space, contemplating. He wore a snake headdress and a snake belt and was accompanied by two felines. Symbols of rainbows appeared in his attire. The mountain was often in the form of a hand, the knuckles representing peaks. These also symbolised the phallic symbol. The counterpart, or possibly the other aspect of the Sky God, was the active God of the snake belt extension. He was either shown with animal elements or engaged in fighting monsters. The Sky God was in fact a dual god.

The Moche were succeeded by the Chimu from about 1000 -

1476 AD. They were potters and the first metallurgists. They were famous craftsmen and later transplanted to Cusco. Their pottery was black and grey, but less interesting than the Mochian. They were also competent weavers. Their motives were similar to the Mochians, although 200 years separated these two cultures. Unfortunately, only a few of their textiles have survived, as saltpetre in the soil destroyed the fabrics. Feathers too were an important element in those far off days, but have almost entirely disappeared. Chimu culture was preceded by Wari and Chavin culture from 700 to 1000 AD.

We saw the small Gold Exhibition, before quickly glancing into the Inca rooms. The Incas were warriors and used the tomi knife universally, and also as a purely ceremonial emblem. It was often incorporated in the headdress of the warrior. Their ceramic, which was cruder and less expressive than the preceding pottery, showed checkboard and step patterns. They used the Ata-ata, which means 'extended arm', to throw their spears, or slings to throw stones. They carried square shields for protection. Big arybollus storage jars appeared, with conical bottoms. Drinking cups fashioned from silver or wood have also been found. Temples had straw roofs, but also bore stepped styled combs made from ceramics.

We briefly glanced at a model of Machu Picchu made to scale before we left.

Our morning's outing completed, we once again strolled across the sunny square of the Plaza de Armas and sat outside a coffee-houses sipping their excellent brew. They all used Gaggia machines and gave the customer the choice of coffee with hot water, which consisted of a strong essence requiring dilution, coffee with hot milk, espresso, cappuccino. We sat and watched the world go by, when we were suddenly informed that our plane to Trujillo was due to leave earlier than we had been told. Hurriedly we walked through crowded streets so that Ruth could catch a glimpse of the Torre Tagle Palace.

We boarded our coach with just enough gear for one night's stop. Planes in Peru are never on time. This applied to our flight to Trujillo too. However, finally, we left Lima and flew above the

Lima Cathedral.

Pyramid of the Moon (Trujillo).

Chimu sculpture (Chan Chan).

clouds to our destination.

Trujillo is a coastal town and presented an excellent centre to explore three pre-Inca cultures: Mocha, Chimu and Wari. It is a true oasis town, founded by Pizzaro, called after his place of birth in Spain. It is a graceful town, with handsome colonial buildings, with many old churches and with the Andes rising in full magnificence in the background. Our hotel was pure Spanish, with gracious lofty rooms downstairs surrounding a small courtyard. Once again, our room faced the square.

We had time to stroll around before dinner. It seemed a happy, active town. We were not certain about the schooling. Too many children of school age were about during school hours for schooling to be truly universal. We actually saw many queuing outside a school next day. Whether space was limited or there were too few teachers, we never found out. It was a city of young people; in fact it was a university town. We noted that the Peruvians appeared to queue for everything. Every public office had a queue and everybody who worked, queued for their weekly pay.

It rained heavily through the night, but sunshine greeted us next morning. We set off by coach to the Moche Valley. Our local guide was a very enthusiastic Peruvian, well known for his local knowledge of archaeology and also an artist in his own right. We later saw his woodcuts of the temples, but there was no time to decide which one to buy. The Moche Valley is extremely fertile, since it is well irrigated, utilising the river of the same name. They grow sugar and maize amongst other things. We stopped to watch adobe bricks being made. The clay was cut and mixed with water and straw and poured into wooden shapes. These were left to dry in the sun for one week and after that they were ready to be used. In olden days only water was added to the clay giving a firmer structure. The man in charge of this particular site was building a house for himself and his family. Beams were used for a gabled roof, which was thatched with reeds.

At one point, a young local boy boarded our bus with ancient pottery to sell. We bought a black jar, supposedly made in Inca times. The lines were smooth and pleasant, both to the eye and to the touch.

Only the brim was slightly chipped.

We continued our journey, which brought us to the Pyramid of the Sun opposite to the Pyramid of the Moon. Between these two lay a vast stretch of nothingness, wasteland. This area had served as a burial ground and had been systematically, inch by inch, searched for artifacts. Nothing was left except desolation. I did manage to find a small shard. There were numerous shells strewn around, evidence that once upon a time the sea had covered this stretch of land. The Temple of the Moon had been built against the White Mountain. Both pyramids had been built of adobe brick and probably had borne a temple on top. Looters had dug a tunnel into the Pyramid of the Moon to look for treasures, but nothing had been found. We followed down the narrow shaft on our bellies and got a view of the magnificent workmanship which had gone into the construction so many years ago. Each adobe brick bore a sign, equivalent to the master symbols found in the masonry in Persepolis, Iran. Several villages would have been detailed to make a certain number of bricks and each village had its own symbol. Literally millions of bricks were used to construct these pyramids.

The sun had risen into a brilliantly blue sky. We walked across the graveyard and climbed up to the flat top of the Pyramid of the Sun. We had a perfect view of the valley of the Moche. The decline was steep and narrow, but we all managed to clamber down to board the coach again to return to Trujillo. On our way, we stopped at a little village to sample the local drink of Chicha, which is made from maize. A delicious drink, akin to our rough cider. It was poured from a big gourd into small ones, resembling wine-tasting cups, and served. Yet another unexpected surprise awaited us back at the hotel. A long table had been prepared in the courtyard for a typical Peruvian meal. To complete our pleasure, we were entertained by four dancers and a small local band. There was a choice of stuffed avocado pear, which was quite excellent, or marinated raw fish, which was equally delicious. This was followed by a rice dish, lightly spiced, containing various ingredients which were not easy to define. I liked it in spite of its somewhat mushy texture. We finished with pancakes with caramel sauce, followed as always, by a choice of tea or coffee.

Refreshed, we set off once more. We managed to visit two beautiful colonial houses before we continued our journey back into pre-Inca time. Both houses were now used as banks and therefore well preserved. They were built in Spanish style with all rooms leading off a cool courtyard. There was some elaborate furniture and glass on display, but time was short and we were unable to linger for too long.

We drove out of town again, this time to see the amazing citadel of the Chimus, called Chan-Chan. Only the adobe walls, some of which bore beautiful carvings, had remained. We saw the walking condor, a bird very much venerated by the Chimus, as was the pelican. We admired the pelican in flight and again in abstract form, depicted without legs and without wings. Only the ground-plan of nine great citadels existed, each of which was a compound built by successive kings. Nine-metre high perimeter walls surround the sacred quarters, with only narrow entrances into the sacred place. None of the entrances were in alignment anywhere, therefore the citadel was most efficiently protected and easier to defend. The whole compound of these nine citadels was surrounded by a high wall. Each citadel had a huge walk-in well, which tapped ground water. Each complex had a burial mound. On the death of each king, his women were sacrificed and buried with him in the mound, along with all his worldly goods. Recently, fifteen skeletons of young women had been found in one mound.

This vast area, covering twenty-eight square kilometres, was quite extraordinary, unlike anything I had ever seen. One had to appreciate the ground-plan and let one's imagination do the rest.

We continued on to the Dragon Temple, also known as the Rainbow Temple. This was the remains of Wari culture, a square adobe structure, which reminded me vaguely of the Cerro Temple outside Mexico City. We walked round it, admiring the strange carvings of gods and dragons. We went up a ramp to the flat top, which gave us a fine view over the valley. On either side of the platform were deep storage spaces. Alongside the ramp ran the deeply gouged Chicha channel for this to be poured down as an offering to the gods.

Time was running out, since our plane was due to leave at 5.15 to take us back to Lima. We paid a quick visit to a fishing village, where we saw the typical reed boats for the first time, reminiscent of the papyrus boats which we had seen on Lake Tana in Ethiopia. After a short time, we were speeding towards the airport, only to be told that there was a delay and we would not leave until 8 pm. We returned to Trujillo and spent the waiting time very profitably. We followed some of our party into Aladdin's Cave, where two of them bought a leather pouffe, which served as an additional valise, while we just looked on. We left our fellow travellers and walked through narrow streets teaming with life, and looked at shops, trying to find a coffee bar, which we located in a narrow lane. We had an excellent cup of coffee and a cake in the cool bar. Rested, we meandered off and finally went into the cathedral on the square, where youngsters began to strum their string instruments, ready to start their pop concert - a scene which I found rather touching and reassuring. We returned to the hotel where we treated ourselves to the local drink of Pisco sour. This is not unlike the well-known snowball. Finally we were on our way to the airport. Content and well satisfied with all we had seen, we reached our hostel, where, in spite of the delay, a meal was waiting for us. We caught a glimpse of a matador in full regalia, before we turned in for the night.

We were up early, ready to pack for our next lap: Cuzco, the ancient capital of the Incas, high up in the Andes. We strolled around the now familiar streets round our hotel until it was time to leave. Inevitably the flight was delayed. I do not think that Aero-Peru is ever on time. The flight was short, just over the hour. We saw the beautiful mountains and the red roofs of Cuzco before we landed. We had been told to walk slowly across the tarmac to the waiting taxis avoiding any exertion.

Having reached the waiting cars, we were immediately besieged by children proffering their wares: mainly sets of llamas, alpachas, vicunas in brass and also attractive dolls in local dress. At this point we all resisted temptation, eager to reach our hotel. Soon we were off to the centre of Cuzco to the Hostel Wiraquoche. We did as we had been told to do and rested on our beds for two hours, having drunk the special herb tea on our arrival.

We loved our stay in Cuzco. It was an unique place - the scenery was superb, whichever way we glanced, and every step took us back into history. The Plaza de Armas, the centre of the city, had been the main square of the Inca capital, surrounded by their palaces. Wherever we looked we saw the remnants of the magnificent Inca walls incorporated into every building. These fantastic walls were built from cornered stones, finely bevelled and exquisitely fitted on each other without cement or mortar of any kind.

Our whole party met at 4 pm for an 'Orientation Walk' with Leonora, a little old lady, our local guide. She was working for her Ph.D. in English or History; whatever her subject was, she had been unable to achieve it. She did speak English, but in her excitement and enthusiasm she lapsed into Spanish from time to time, leaving our tour leader the task of translating.

The indigenous population of Cuzco are mainly of Indian descent; short and squat, broad shouldered, with sharp features and fine brown complexion. It was most difficult to distinguish the sexes by their features or statures. Men and women alike had finely chiselled features, both were short and broad, both carried heavy burdens. These were either the wares which they wished to sell or heavy loads of firewood, or their small children. Children were carried on their mother's back in a colourful strip of woven cloth and were suckled on the breast until the next baby arrived. Characteristically, the women wore white, tall straw hats, which made them look even more mannish. They wore short skirts, which were almost kilts, with numerous petticoats beneath. From early morning until late at night they sat on the ground, sometimes on top of their bundles, trying to sell their wares, which were spread out around them. They sat and knitted or walked along spinning their famous alpaca wool. Life in Cuzco never failed to amaze us. Music was everywhere, either the lilting sound of flutes or the soft tones issuing from the strange, bellied string instruments.

We went to the local market, which was partly under cover and partly on the street near the station. Everything which anyone wanted or needed could be bought here. Women sat surrounded by

Placa da Armas (Cusco).

their meagre produce of fruit and eggs. There were small grocery stalls selling pasta of varying kinds, excellent coffee, finely pulverised, and special herb tea, which is supposed to combat the effects of the high altitude. Everywhere knitwear in pure alpaca wool and lovely fleecy blankets and colourful stoles were thrust temptingly at us. All was colourful, discounting the stench, squalor and mud (it had rained each day; even in Trujillo it had rained at night). We learned later that recently the weather had been unusually cold and wet all over Peru.

Our hotel was comfortable; our simple bedroom looked down the Avenue de Sol towards the mountains. We had a small washroom with a shower, which was somewhat unpredictable as far as the hot water was concerned. However, with the help of our universal plug, we managed some kind of bath each day. There was a small snack bar, well used all day long, where we had our breakfast and a dining room downstairs, which produced excellent meals at a painfully slow pace.

We slept little, since at 4.30 am church bells started to ring. Not in unison, but entirely out of step, until 5 am. Therefore I often slipped out on my own to walk across the square early in the morning and to steal quietly into one of the fabulous churches, feeling slightly uncomfortable, since the devout had come to take early mass, whilst I was there merely to look, an intruder into their privacy.

The cathedral, just across from our hotel, was impressive in its colonial architecture. Its main altar was of pure silver. One of its chapels was that of 'The Lord of the Earthquake'. Legend has it that during one of their severe earthquakes the image of the Lord was taken out on the Plaza and the people beseeched it to make the tremors stop. As soon as the image had been carried out into the square, the earthquake stopped. To the right side of the cathedral stands the El Triunfo Church, with its fine stone carving; to the left, the Jesus Maria Church, which is pure baroque and has a most impressive altar carved in silver. The doll-faced statues were all dressed in velvet and lace. One particular group of the Holy Trinity were so childlike in concept that I found it very touching.

In all churches were paintings of the Cusquerian School. These were primitive paintings by Indians, influenced by the Spanish style of the 17th and 18th centuries. Unfortunately they were difficult to see in the dim light. We were to come across many more of these paintings, none of which bore a signature, since the Inquisition forbade Indians to learn to read or write. One of the most famous of these Indian painters, however, always put his signature in the form of a bird somewhere in his picture.

We all ascended one of Cuzco's many steep and narrow lanes, climbing up the lush side of the surrounding hills. Most of the houses, even today, are built of red adobe bricks with overhanging roofs, reminiscent of those we had seen in Cordoba, Mexico. They are covered with convex slates because of the heavy rains during the rainy season. There were no gutters, as we know them; open holes were meant to take the overflow. Unfortunately most of them were full of rubbish. There were also gutters across the street, covered by grids.

Almost every single building in these cobbled lanes stood on Inca foundations. A good deal of restoration was being carried out by Unesco, who had converted the former Seminar of St. Antony, itself a splendid colonial building, into their headquarters. We walked past the House of the Admiral, which was being restored, to the Square of St. Antony, where we 'disbanded'. We slipped into the Unesco headquarters and admired the courtyard from which their offices led. We walked along the gallery to admire the restored wall paintings. It got dark quite suddenly about 6 o'clock and there was little light on the streets to guide us. But it did not prove too difficult to find our way back to the Plaza de Armas. Every town in South America has a Plaza de Armas, which means 'a place for arms', where weapons used to be stored. The Plaza de Armas in Cuzco had been used in Inca times to bring out the mummies of the previous Sapa-Inca from the Temple of the Sun on feast days. They were arranged in rows beside the reigning Inca and homage was paid to them all.

We drove up above town next morning, enjoying the panorama before us as the road climbed higher to take us to the ruined fortress of Sacsahuaman. Although little remained, it was an impressive sight.

Three walls run parallel for over 360 meters and the base of 21 bastions could still be seen. The stones were monumental in size. Here was the enormous parade-ground; carved out of solid rock stood the throne on which the Inca sat to muster his troops. The Incas had an obsession for rocks and whichever Inca remains we visited, we found natural rock incorporated into man-made masonry. I will go further than this - man-made masonry evolved from natural stone formations. Zig-zag channels were chicha-grooves, down which the maize beer flowed during festivals. Up here, the Incas held out for some time in a desperate stand against the Spaniards. It was on this spot, amongst the lush meadows, that we saw our first llamas with red tassels in their ears.

We travelled on to Tambomanchay, which many archaeologists call 'Inn' standing on the Royal Road, leading north. It was a resting place for the Inca who travelled through all four corners of his land. There were some well-proportioned niches visible in the uppermost part of the finely dressed wall. Water still flowed through a hidden channel out of the masonry into the well-preserved Inca's Bath. More remnants of Inca walls stood sentry on the opposite side of this ancient Inca road. We left this pleasant place to visit Ken Ko, an Inca shrine. A fascinating place, partly rugged as Nature willed, partly man-made. It consisted of a limestone crag carved into a multitude of steps and seats of basins and water channels. Amongst them was a zig-zag channel to pour the maize beer down and also to perform oracles. That is why some archaeologists refer to Ken Ko as 'The Labyrinth'. Animal figures, particularly snakes, were carved into the rock. Near the crag stood an amphitheatre, elliptical in shape, surrounded by a stone wall and seats. Below were underground chambers, which housed an altar. A large rock in the centre of the amphitheatre looked, with a little imagination, like a feline creature - a jaguar or puma.

This time no herd of llamas distracted us in our search into the past, but we saw a man weaving with one end of the frame tied to a tree, whilst the other was tied around his waist, just as it was done in the times of the Incas.

We all decided to walk back to town and enjoyed the freedom

of the hills, treading most carefully between the fields of corn, barley, potatoes and beans.

It had been a good morning and we had no difficulty in improvising a snack in our room, before we met up again for our next sightseeing tour. This time we walked down the Calle de Loretto, which had the most magnificent Inca wall, to reach Santa Domingo, a former Dominican convent, built on the ruins of the Coricancha, the Inca Temple of the Sun. Incidentally, in Peru a convent corresponds to our monastery and vice versa, which seemed strange to us. The convent was being restored and excavations were still being carried out, revealing more and more of the original structure. As always, the cloisters exuded an atmosphere of serenity. There were many very intriguing and interesting murals to see as we walked beneath the cool arches. We also admired some very handsomely carved wooden ceilings, which were in the process of being restored and date back to the Spanish era. Wherever we looked, we saw remains of Inca masonry. Various temples, such as The Temple of the Morning Star or the Temple of the Rainbow interconnected by windows, aligned in a straight line. We saw niches which probably housed idols, and a resting place for the Inca's litter. The Inca always travelled in a litter, well curtained off from the rest of the world. He was, after all, the son of the Sun and therefore almost divinity himself. Whoever approached him did so with a bundle on his back, to indicate humility. In this convent, Inca and Spanish architecture became fused. The Temple of the Rainbow with its niches for idols, displayed a colonial carved ceiling. Somewhere in the peaceful cloisters we found stone columns intricately carved by Indian hands. We had learned to recognise Indian craftsmen, since they always incorporated flowers and fruit, birds and beasts in their carvings. Unmistakably an Indian face would suddenly appear side by side with Christian emblems.

The most impressive part of this complex was the Temple of the Sun, with the usual hitching post, a stone peg to which the golden disc was tied, facing the sun. The temple itself had the most perfect circular wall. It is interesting to reflect that these people, who were technically in many respects much advanced (as is evident from the bevelling of these enormous stones and the building of those perfect walls; from their roads and what remains of their irrigation system), were a people who did not know the wheel or the true arch and who had no script. They did, however, have a very complicated accounting system based on knots, the Quipu. Some people were specially trained to interpret and memorise these knots. When looking at some weaving, we noticed the recurrence of certain motifs. Some archaeologists think that these correspond to our heraldic signs. We wondered whether in fact they were not akin to hieroglyphics.

Let me return to our wanderings. We found it easy to orientate ourselves in Peruvian towns. All the ones we visited were laid out in the grid system. As in America, directions were given in blocks.

Our next visit was to the Archaeological Museum, which was firmly closed. Our numbers had by then dwindled to six. We followed our leader and Leonora, our local guide, and visited the Historical Museum instead. It was a pleasant building, formerly the residence of Garcilos de la Vega, the son of an Inca princess and a conquistador, who became a well-known historian of the Inca past.

The sun streamed into the courtyard, which displayed ancient farm implements. Most of the rooms contained Cuzcan paintings and ornate, heavy colonial furniture. Unfortunately, none of us had sufficient knowledge to assess these paintings, which in their simplicity produced a faint echo of the icons we had seen in Russia.

Leonora then took us to see the Church of the Compania, a Jesuit church on the Plaza de Armas, built to outstrip the cathedral in its magnificence, with its dome almost rising above the cathedral. It stood on the Inca site of the Palace of the Serpents. It contained many paintings and fine murals and has six chapels. Leonora wanted to take us into the sacristy, but this was closed. We had to content ourselves with peeping through the large keyhole and admiring the carved figures of two saints. Before returning to our hotel, we embarked on a shopping expedition, which became quite hilarious. Our numbers had shrunk to three: Ruth, myself and a charming American from Boston - Beatrice, 'Bea' for short. She worked for a shipping firm and had a 'computer brain' - everything was catalogued on small filing cards. She was great fun to be with, looking over her half-glasses with pigtails framing her pleasant face. Entirely self-contained, she obviously did not wish to become involved with anyone.

We were set to leave next morning to spend the next two days at Machu Picchu. We had been strongly advised to take food with us. Leonora was only too delighted to be asked for help. We swept through the cobbled streets of Cuzco; first to a special cheese shop to buy a whole round of cheese. Then at rapid speed across the Plaza de Armas, down a side street to a bakery to purchase numerous rounds of flat bread. Back to the Plaza once more, up yet another alleyway to get a bottle or two of wine, and finally shooting off in another direction to locate a stall with a large heap of oranges.

Laden with our goodies we returned to our hotel, but the day was not yet done for us. We packed, leaving our main luggage behind in the hotel, and only taking the minimum of hand luggage with us for the visit to Machu Picchu. To complete the day, we went to see the nightly folklore show at the local theatre: an excellent performance by a competent company of artists in colourful costumes, accompanied by an able band of musicians. Peruvian music is very pleasing, easy on the ears, with a good deal of flute playing.

We rose early next morning. We had been warned to mind our bags, since pick-pockets were a byword in Peru, particularly at railway stations and especially in Cuzco on the Tourist Train to Machu Picchu. Nothing happened and, even more remarkable, the train left on time at 7 o'clock.

We met Oscar on the train. He was a schoolteacher who spent most of his time as a guide. Walking up and down the train, he gave a running commentary on the exciting scenery, whilst a great deal of activity took place on the train. Vendors appeared offering paperbags of potato chips, Inca Cola, tea or coffee and postcards. It was a very remarkable journey, since the long train, which had to be shunted four times in a zig-zag fashion, encircled the town and then climbed up the steepest slope. Without the help of the shunting engines, it would not have been able to negotiate the steep gradient.

Machu Picchu lies 42 km beyond Cuzco at an altitude of 2,280 meters, whilst Cuzco itself lies at 3,500 meters. It was quite a journey, leading over a pass and travelling through fertile valleys surrounded by the wood-clad mountains of the Andes. We followed the turbulent river Urubamba with its water stained red from the soil. Many crystal-clear streams joined it from the side valleys. We passed the entrance to the Inca's sacred valley with well-preserved terraces clearly visible to either side. The scenery varied between fields of barley and maize, meadows full of flowers with cacti here and there and with willow trees gently dipping into the water. We passed peacefully grazing cattle and drove through little woods. In a clearing stood a big stone with a wooden cross beside it and a wreath in the tree up above. The big stone no doubt stirred the Inca veneration for rocks; to compromise the cross was placed beside it. Many houses bear a simple cross on their roofs, usually flanked by small cow-like animal statues to either side. I cannot help feeling that the Indians still believe in their ancient tradition, but combine this with their devout Catholicism.

We had reached our destination at the end of the valley by midday and caught our first glimpse of Machu Picchu towering high above. Six buses stood ready and waiting to take the eager tourists up the steep zig-zag road to this famous site. No sooner had we stepped off the train, than we were surrounded by little girls trying to sell alpaca pullovers, chains made from shells, embroidered bags and many other things. They spoke English well and were extremely persistent in their efforts to sell.

We were soon seated on a bus, admiring the lush vegetation as we climbed higher and higher to reach the Tourist Hotel, which originally was the base camp for the archaeologists who excavated the site. We sat in the sun and shared our cheese and wine with some members of our party. We spent the rest of the day exploring the ruins of Machu Picchu, a unique and most impressive site of staircases, temples, palaces, towers and fountains straddling the majestic heights at the end of the valley through which the Urubamba river flows.

The city was divided into well-defined quarters. We entered the agricultural area with terrace upon terrace where they used to grow maize - their staple diet - many varieties of potatoes and other necessities of Inca life.

Machu Picchu.

We explored the royal tombs below an enormous rock and walked through the artisans' quarters up to the Temple of the Three Windows. Wherever we looked were flowers in wild profusion: gladioli, irises, violets, dahlias and many orchids. Small humming birds flitted past us. We looked down into the Urubamba Valley where we had come from, to one side of the saddle where we stood, and down into the valley of the river Vilanota, which was temporarily closed by a landslide, to the other side.

About half a dozen of us took the Inca Trail to climb the steep peak of the Huayna Picchu. It was extremely hot and the ascent quite arduous. I reached the top and stood talking to an American who had finished high school and had decided to take a year off before going on to university. He had been working with a river company in Chile and was now exploring Peru before returning to study geology. We met many young people, mainly Americans and Canadians, who were pleasant to talk to. They usually travelled on their own, but had a kind of bush telegraph which told them which trail to take, the best overnight stops and where you could eat cheaply and well. My young American friend had sat on top of Huayna Picchu for the best part of an hour, at peace with the world, reading a book. He was getting ready for his descent, since dark clouds had begun to gather on the horizon. Ruth had not accompanied me on my climb, but had wandered up to the highest temple of the city, where she too had become engaged in conversation with a young traveller who hailed from Canada. He had reached Machu Picchu following the ancient Inca Trail from Cuzco and had spent the night curled up snugly in his sleeping-bag in the temple.

We all returned to the Tourist Hotel, a primitive abode, where the water was turned off between two and six pm and again between eleven and seven am. Electricity too was cut off during these hours. The meal was poor. It had to be carried into the dining room up some steps from an outside kitchen. To complicate matters, each course was served in individual dishes, therefore it was a precarious and lengthy business to be served a three-course meal with coffee to follow. Tea or coffee were always included.

We were a happy party, talking and laughing. Nothing could

mar the sense of excitement and elation, nor disturb the atmosphere of mystery which prevailed. This site had escaped the Spaniards and laid hidden for many years, until an American, Hiram Bingham, was led there by an Indian in 1911. It was then explored by an archaeological expedition from Yale University, who found a large number of skeletons, with females outweighing the males. One of the theories put forward was, that the Virgins of the Sun had fled into the mountains after the sacking of Cuzco. The Virgins of the Sun were known as Mamma Cuna. They were girls of special beauty and trained in special convents. Some of them became servants of the temple, others were given to nobles as wives. Some were probably offered up as sacrifices. Few returned home. They used to weave the fine vicuna cloth, used for the temples and to clothe the great Inca himself. Other archaeologists hold different views about Machu Picchu.

The zig-zag road leading to Machu Picchu has been named Bingham Way. He also wrote a book, called The Last City of the Incas, which I have not read.

I had had great plans for the morning and had hoped to watch the sun rise over Machu Picchu. But it rained relentlessly all through the night and when I rose and stepped outside, heavy mist concealed the mountains. Fortunately the rain stopped eventually, the clouds lifted and we were able to go back to the site for the rest of the morning. We had to abandon our intention to follow one of the Inca Trails. It was far too wet underfoot and the visibility was poor. But we had a marvellous time climbing up the wonderfully preserved terraces, most of which were overgrown by a luxuriant variety of wild plants. I collected quite a few of the various species and Ruth photographed some of the orchids.

We visited the highest temple from which we overlooked the whole complex. As on every Inca site, in Machu Picchu we found the big stone with hewn steps and the hitching post. We wandered up and down many stairs, through corridors and courtyards, up from temple to temple. On one of these temples, standing high up on the mountain, we met an Indian family enjoying a picnic lunch. They asked us to take photographs. First the baby was placed (rather precariously) on the altarstone, after which the whole family assembled to be taken as a group. We promised to send them a print if it turned out well. Their address was simply 'care of the Post Office, Machu Picchu'.

Time had come to leave this enchanted place. We finished our wine and bread sitting outside the hotel. Some of us decided to walk down, whilst the rest elected to wait for buses. We set off at a brisk trot since time was running short. I suddenly realised that I had not got my precious plants. I turned sharply and sprinted back to the hotel. I saw some strange animals cross my path - big round eyes, set in a monkey-like face peered at me from thick undergrowth. There were about half a dozen or so of these funny creatures with long, striped tails. I was told that they were lemurs. Beatrice had taken care of my plants. I turned on my heel and walked fast to catch up with the rest of the party, regretting that there was no time to linger. The scenery was so lovely, the flowers beautiful. I was sorry that I failed to get a wild begonia nor a wild geranium, both of which grow in profusion. However, I picked up a clump of orchids which someone had abandoned.

We all reached the train with ten minutes to spare. Ruth used the time to buy a most attractive alpaca cardigan from a little girl. As soon as we had boarded the train, the little girl with her wares followed and literally had to be bundled off as we drew out of the station. There was only one train, leaving Cuzco at seven am, returning from Machu Picchu at three pm.

The journey was pleasant. Oscar reappeared and so did the cans of Inca Cola, beakers of tea and coffee, trays with sandwiches and potato chips. A couple in our party sat opposite an Indian family of mother, grandmother and two children. The baby was fed without any break from the beginning of the journey to the end. First on the breast, then with some fruit and back to the breast again. Poor Sir Roy hid behind a book; Lady Kate was much amused.

Watching the scenery slip past was an unending pleasure. There is no twilight: night descends quite suddenly at six pm. The moon hangs 'upside down'.

Back in Cuzco we all met up after dinner and had a spirited

discussion about the Incas. The leader of our party had been ill up in Machu Picchu, but had recovered sufficiently by the time we had reached our hostel, to chair the after-dinner gathering. Fortunately we found our packed suitcases exactly as we had left them in the room we had occupied before.

The next day was free for us to do as we pleased, to give everybody a chance to recover from our hectic tour. Fortunately we both felt very fit, but many of our party suffered from various complaints. I do not recollect a single day when all was well with everyone. They were indeed a motley collection, but that is quite a different story.

We had a busy day, which we thoroughly enjoyed. We had intended to go to see the Archaeological Museum. On the way there we bought two tapes of the enchanting Peruvian music. The girl in the shop kindly played them for us before we bought them. When we arrived at the museum, which bore a notice that it was open from seven am to midday, we found it firmly closed. We knocked and knocked until eventually a sullen youth appeared reluctantly and wrote down on a piece of paper that the hours of opening were now from ten o'clock until midday. In fact, the museum remained completely closed for the next two days.

We wandered through the narrow, cobbled streets, catching a glimpse of small workshops as we walked along. We found a little knitwear shop, where we bought a pullover for each of us, since it was quite chilly in the early mornings. Determined not to miss anything, we looked for and found the Museum de Artes, which was housed in the former Archbishop's Palace. It was a lovely building with a cool courtyard, where all rooms led off the tiled corridor which surrounded it. It contained Cuzcan paintings of religious subjects and heavy Spanish furniture which was very ornate.

Before returning to our hostel for a light midday snack, we changed some travellers cheques. No bank dealt with foreign currency.

In the afternoon we set off once again on our wanderings. This time we tried to get some walking shoes for myself, since my trusty walking shoes of many years' standing had finally disintegrated. It took some time to find the right size and then to convince the saleslady that I required two shoes of the same size for both my feet. She seemed very willing to serve, but did not seem very bright. Finally, however, we walked out of the shop with me triumphantly wearing a most comfortable pair of shoes, which stood me in good stead for the rest of the trip.

We looked in vain for silverware to buy. The really nice articles were too expensive.

We next visited an exhibition of watercolours by a local artist in the official tourist office, which was a magnificent hall adjacent to the church La Compania de Jesus on Plaza de Armas. Needless to say, we could not resist and bought one of the paintings, although it bore no price and the little lady in charge had no idea how much it might be, but hoped that the artist himself would reappear. He did surface and we clinched the deal.

The noble building on the other side of La Compania was being used for public entertainment. There were always long queues waiting outside the imposing door, for it to open. I think it was usually a filmshow which was being shown. Next door to this hall stood the university, with a sunny courtyard and poorly furnished lecture rooms. The number of students struck us as small and composed of widely differing age groups.

By that time siesta had finished, life began to return and streets began to fill again. We left the Plaza de Armas, walked along the narrow street of Santa Catalina to visit the cloisters of the same name. These belonged to a closed order. Visitors were able to buy gifts - which the nuns had made - through a grill in the entrance hall. Having chosen, they then placed the money on a turn-table and received the sweets or toys in return. It was an extraordinary visit since our guide did not speak English and made it her main task to put on lights and turn them off again, shepherding us in the right direction. The cloisters were cool, exuding the usual air of serenity. We found once again the now-familiar Cuzcan paintings, as well as hand-embroidered priceless vestments, silver chalices of intricate workmanship and other treasures of the Church. The chapel was quite lovely, with splendid carvings and almost Rembrandt-like paintings of sombre, vibrant hues. There were so many of them that they were placed high up under the lofty roof. At the back of the church a grill separated the nuns from the rest of the congregation. Each church we had visited contained one, sometimes two, wooden wheels with bells which were rung at Christmas time. They were in this church too.

The highlight of this visit was a little chapel, completely covered in murals, which were divided into three registers. The topmost was devoted to the story of the saints, the middle one (almost Watteau-like in style) depicted the pleasures of the flesh, and the lowermost represented a garland of flowers. I certainly had never seen anything like this before. We tried to get a slide, or at least a postcard, but 'mañana' was the sweet reply.

We walked through the deserted streets of Cuzco to a rather dilapidated building in the evening, where, in a simple hall, we were shown some slides of the Inca Trail from Cuzco to Machu Picchu, compiled by an architect. Some views were excellent, others were projected up on the ceiling rather than on the screen, but we appreciated the kind thought of putting on this show specially for us.

Having replenished our provisions, we set off next morning to visit the Sacred Valley of the Incas. This time we followed the river Urubamba by road. Soon we stopped to watch llamas, sheep and goats, as well as the inevitable pig being driven along by their shepherds. These were followed by boys carrying the 'digging stick'. Digging sticks were used before the Incas, but the Incas added a crossbar for the foot and as such they are still used.

Our next stop was a tiny hamlet where we were surrounded by friendly children. Part of the humble adobe huts stood on the river bank, the rest climbed up the steep mountainside. The cows negotiated the crude mud steps climbing daintily to their respective homes.

We crossed the river and drove through the village of Pisac, which struck us as very poor and miserable. An Indian market takes place on the central square each Sunday morning. This, I believe, forms a great tourist attraction. Sadly, even the little church on the square looked forsaken and decayed.

We left Pisac behind and climbed higher, looking back on the Sacred Valley. High above us were the familiar signs of Inca habitation: fine terraces, some still in use, walls and towers. Our bus came to a sudden halt. A landslide barred our way. We had intended to climb up to explore and cross the saddle to descend into the next valley, where we would have joined our bus. We had to be content to scramble up the stony path to see three quarters of this old Inca fortress, walk along the saddle, before returning the way we had come, down to the Urubamba Valley.

The site itself had numerous temples, chambers, storage rooms and the usual huaca meaning sacred stones. The climb was steep, the view magnificent. As always flowers grew in wild profusion, especially orange and deep blue irises of the dwarf variety and wild lupins.

We retraced our steps, admiring the lush meadows in the valley. We drove through Pisac, by which time some Indians were sitting in the street, offering poor-looking fruit for sale. We did not stop, but continued through sunny countryside until we stopped at a wayside hostel which advertised all kind of modern amenities. Here we watched two men operating a chainsaw, quite ingeniously, to saw big treetrunks.

The hostel itself certainly possessed potential. The old part, a former hacienda, lay around two courtyards. There was a splendid dining-room with pseudo-colonial furniture. Two bedrooms looked inviting, with their simple but handsome carved furniture and shower room en suite. Sadly the kitchen resembled a dungeon and was very primitive. We sat in the sunny courtyard sipping delicious fruit juice. We were shown the new part. Through a small, rather neglected vegetable patch we came into a meadow, which had rustic tables and stools dotted about made from tree trunks and crude planks. A small swimming pool was being built. The new bedrooms, some still under construction, were simple, with adjacent shower rooms. The manager or owner spoke perfect English, but had a marked continental accent. In fact he came from Czechoslovakia and had been running the hotel for the past eight years. He had married the

Spanish lady who owned the hacienda. After the Land Reform, all land had been taken away, and in order to survive he had converted the family home into an inn. However, the present cooking facilities were not entirely satisfactory for European demands.

We continued our journey along the Urumbaba river until we reached another hotel, called Nacanjahaco. This appeared to be well established. Some of our party chose from the menu and sat in the shade on an open veranda. The rest of us settled on the grass near a pool and ate our picnic. It was incredibly peaceful in spite of a noisy parrot watching us from the branches of a tree. The hostel seemed to be well equipped and efficiently run by the young manager, who spoke perfect English, being half Peruvian and half English.

Refreshed, we continued our journey. On our right, the mountains grew in height until we saw the snow-covered peak of Mount Chicho. We stopped along our way to look at some royal tombs, carved high into the rocks. The Incas were most insistent that their dead should enjoy a beautiful view, and always made certain that there was free access to their departed. They were truly horrified at the Christian idea of burial below ground.

We drove through the village of Ollantaitambo (tambo means inn) at the end of the valley to reach the ruins of the old and most impressive Inca fortress temple. We walked through a courtyard and then ascended steeply up numerous steps hewn into the mountainside. We followed a staircase in the centre with terraces either side, up to lofty heights. We reached a plateau with the familiar hitching post and a stone throne. We came upon a curious block of granite, vertical and smooth, divided into three sections. No one quite knew whether this was an altar divided into three or not. High above this plateau were more walls and the remains of further buildings. I climbed further up, found a small shell and dug up some orchids to bring home.

Well-preserved remnants of a garrison were visible on the opposite mountainside. In fact, Ollantaitambo was successfully defended by Manco Inco warriors against Hernando Pizarro in 1536.

Some children had attached themselves to us. One particularly persistent little boy asked for a pen. I promised him one, as soon as we had returned to our bus. I kept my promise. We did not leave at that point, but went in search of the Princess' Bath, which consisted of a small granite basin tucked away in a field. Clear water flowed into it. We strolled through lovely meadows, faithfully followed by the little boy. We came to a grand rock cliff, soaring high into the blue sky. Steps, platforms, shapes and faces were carved into it. We climbed high up it, but my little companion outdid us all. nimbly as a mountain goat he gaily skipped up and lightly jumped down again, caught us up and presented me with some plants. I was touched, having told him to stop being a 'pest' when he followed us, not realising that he wanted to thank me for my gift and having noticed my obsession with plants intended to add to my collection.

We stopped in the village of Ollantaitambo and parked in the market place to walk through the narrow lanes. This little place was built in the exact way the Incas used to build their towns. Stones from the original Inca city had been used to construct the village. Each house was entirely enclosed behind walls. Humans and livestock shared the yard and the rooms which led off the yard. It seemed all very primitive and we ourselves felt rather like animals in the zoo, being watched at every step we took.

When we returned to our coach, a lorry packed to full capacity with human cargo was leaving the market place, bound for Cuzco I think. Well satisfied with our day we returned to Cuzco ourselves.

We rose early next morning. I took Ruth to see the Church of Santa Clara, which was most extraordinary, since the whole of the interior was decorated in mirrorwork. We also went to visit La Merced, which contained children's toys in a glass case. The nuns were singing sweetly behind the grill. We never managed to visit the cloisters, which apparently were quite beautiful and possessed a world-famous monstrance among their treasures. I had been to these churches by myself on my early morning wanderings through the town. I had also been to San Pedro, close to the station, where once again I had found the richness of the altar and the profusion of paintings quite dazzling. I had quietly stolen into the Church of San Frances and had admired the magnificent carvings of choir and pulpit. I had also slipped into the Church of Santa Theresa, which had a magnificent golden altar. Nearby stood the graceful statue of Garcilos de la Vega, the historian. One morning I had wandered far afield on my way to the Church of San Bezen at the southern outskirts of the town. My path led through the Indian quarters. Life was stirring, people were opening their little shops. Tailors were setting up their hand-operated sewing machines, the baker was sweeping the floor, the smithy stoking his fire. The little bars were beginning to lay out food and drinks. All was rather dirty and poor. I reached a railway bridge and stood rooted to the ground. Along the railway lines lived Indians in incredible, indescribable filth and poverty. I tried to get a closer look, but could not make myself go down the stairs. The stench of human misery was quite unbearable. It is useless for any of my friends to tell me, 'But you knew that there was poverty in Peru', or 'you have seen poverty before'. In Peru, all human dignity appears to have been lost, abject acceptance and apathy rules. Maybe I was wrong in my assessment, but certainly this was the impression I received, standing on that railway bridge. I tried to convey this to Ruth. Together we walked to the bridge and stood in silence. From here we could see the twin towers of the church of Bezen (Bethlehem). I had walked up to it, crossed the little park in front of it, where I had seen a young boy carrying a parrot on his arm. This church had been built by the Indians and had a splendid main altar in silver and, as usual, was rich in paintings from the Cuzcan school.

We met up with our group to visit the Archaeological Museum, which was open this time. We had a very pleasant local guide. Unfortunately our group was too large, crowding into the small museum which consisted only of a few rooms. Leading off a cobbled courtyard, it was well displayed with some interesting exhibits. I was particularly intrigued by small prototypes of buildings, castles and temples, cast in clay. Whether these served the architects as models or not, no one knew. Equally fascinating was their custom of placing their star-shaped metal weapons on the branch of a tree and letting the branch grow into it, so that it was firmly secured and could not be used as a deadly weapon. Their pride and joy were forty miniature turquoise figures found in Piquillacta. We visited the mummy room which held some remarkable mummies, complete with hair, teeth and nails. In this room also hung some interesting historic paintings and some exquisite textiles, neatly displayed. As with all museums, it really would have taken more than one cursory visit to appreciate all which was there to be seen.

We returned to our hostel and found that young Lucinda had organised an expedition to follow the Inca Trail. We decided to join and eleven of us set off on this adventure. We walked past the many street vendors, past the renaissance facade of La Merced, through the arch which spanned the road and, no doubt, was once the city gate. We walked past the wrought iron gate of Santa Clara of the mirrors, strolled through the bustling market near the railway station and started climbing. But after a short while Lucinda thought that we had taken the wrong direction. We retraced our steps and started walking through some other narrow lanes, catching glimpses of courtyards and small shops. We found a steep, cobbled street, which led us to the church of Santa Anna, with its tower standing on its own. It may be that, as in Norway, this too was used in case of fire to ring the bell. This little street was most interesting. Tiny shops sold most elaborate candles; most houses had special runs for guinea-pigs in the backs of their small rooms. A herd of llamas trotted uphill behind us. Apparently, when crossed, they will spit. This time, however, children spat at them.

Once we had got beyond the town, we sat at the grass verge and shared our lunch. After a short rest, we continued, following the road, which climbed up in easy stages. We passed few houses. We were told that wherever there was a stick festooned with paper flowers, there was a bar selling Chicha and Inca Cola. We passed many of them, but did not stop to buy a drink, sharing some orange juice instead to quench our thirst.

Soon the first of us fell back. Susan, Lucinda's cousin, a strange young woman, turned on her heels and returned to base. Later Frances, a thryrotoxic widow, decided she had had enough. She rested for a while amongst the meadows and pigs before she hailed a taxi back to town. Finally, two Welsh civil servants decided to strike their own trail and headed north. The rest of us plodded on. The trail we followed led eventually to Equador, rather a long walk for an afternoon. We changed directions and, leaving the road, followed a single track railway line for a little while, before deciding to head back to Cuzco across the hills. It was rough going, but finally we saw the ruins of Sacsahuaman rising majestically in the distance. We knew now exactly where Cuzco lay. But we missed the path and had to negotiate a number of deep gullies, meadows and many fields, before finally reaching a river-bed which led us back to town. We walked through isolated small-holdings, asking our way. We passed some woodcutters with transistors by their sides. I think transistors must have recently arrived, since we had found them at most extraordinary places: people walking sedately along would play them, and even up at Machu Picchu we had heard them amongst the ruins. We did enjoy the views of meadows, mountains, woods of dark hue and in-between the gentle bluish grey colour of newly planted eucalyptus trees. We reached home feeling elated, almost like pioneers.

  I tried in vain to visit the church of Santa Blas up on the hill. I had been in the early morning and found it closed, then too. But on my way up to the church, I had been tempted to step inside a small art gallery. The pictures were quite lovely, mostly portraits of Indian faces. I met Beatrice, our American fellow traveller, and took her to see the paintings. She was equally enthralled and bought a picture of a flute player.

  Later that evening we went to yet another slideshow in the same dilapidated hall as we had been to before. This time the slides were mainly of pottery from the various cultures we had seen. They were quite excellent and Ian, our tour leader, and the curator from the Archaeological Museum of Cuzco, gave most stimulating commentaries.

  Next day we set off for Cuicuero, which means in old Quechu language, 'He who does everything'. It lies approximately 12,000 ft high and took two hours' pleasant drive through well-cultivated countryside. On the way we saw an experimental industrial development. I think it was a cement factory. In order to attract the higher executives, provisions were being made for childrens' playgrounds and schools. We had noticed both playgrounds and schools on our way up to Machu Picchu. We passed a field where farmers were busily using their Taklea (digging stick) to turn the soil to plant potatoes. The potato is a native of Peru and there exist many varieties. The poor women on the market graded them by size, colour and shape and sorted them into neat little piles. Up in the mountains they also grew a cereal called quinon. This took the place of rice and corn, since it grew well at higher levels. It looked like millet.

We left the road and followed a track which was very muddy, owing to all the rain we had had. A van delivering Inca Cola barred our way. It had got bogged down, trying to turn. With all hands on deck, it was dislodged and we were able to proceed. However, when we reached the village, part of the road had been washed away. We left our coach and walked on foot to the lovely Inca remains. Suddenly the village women appeared on the grassy courtyard, spreading their colourful wares on the green carpet, tempting us to buy. We did buy a very attractive queros, which is a gaily painted wooden goblet. Later, just as we were about to board the bus, Ruth, with Ian's help, bought a wooden spindle complete with a ball of wool, which an old lady who had been standing watching us climb on the coach, was twisting into two-ply strands.

Chichero was pure enchantment. The grassy square was separated from an old medieval church by superb Inca walls with many niches. It was surrounded by three terraces for spectators. No doubt, the square served as ceremonial place. We descended some steps and passed along a corridor. It was easy to follow the ground-plan, consisting of many rooms. Each room had been supplied with water. A perfect drainage system had been installed. The walls were built of dry stone: no cement had been used. We found evidence of plaster tucked away in two corners. No one knew whether this complex served as palace, residence or temple. Beyond these rooms and corridors was the most fascinating labyrinth, reminiscent of Ken-Ko with its many steps, stone seats, channels and caves and the zigzags. The view down beyond the craggy rocks into the fertile valley was breathtakingly beautiful. Unfortunately, time did not permit us to visit the church, which had delightful murals, even on its external walls. We were anxious to return to Cuzco in time for another journey, this time to the south of the city.

On our way back we stopped to watch a couple setting up a waft in the same way as their forefathers had done. They had chosen the outside wall of a factory producing fertiliser.

On our morning trip to Chichero we had escaped Oscar, our official guide, since he had not appeared as arranged. In Chichero Ian had found a 'social worker' willing and able to act as local guide, in return for a free ride back to Cuzco.

In the afternoon we headed south. Soon we arrived at a lake which had threatened to flood the surrounding villages. The inhabitants of one of them had resisted all efforts to be resettled on higher ground. They lived a miserable existence in a swamp village. In fact, on our return journey we discovered a second swamp village.

Regretfully we passed the entrance to the Monkey Temple, but there was not sufficient time to visit it. We went off the road to the mystery village of Piquillacta, a large compound surrounded by high walls. The path we followed must have been the main street. According to most archaeologists, this site dated back to pre-Inca times and stemmed from Wari culture, 600 - 800 AD. Some authorities claim that it served as a mere storage depot for the army, others think it was a resting station on the way from Cuzco to Lake Titicaca. Either explanation appeared strange to us, since the whole complex was vast and built to a definite street plan. Some of the walls had strange protuberances, which no one could explain.

We left this place of mystery behind us and continued south. We passed the remains of an Inca wall, which obviously had been built across the road to form a checkpoint along the way. We finally arrived at Andahuaylillas. The extremely attractive square had been restored and was surrounded by handsome colonial buildings. The church, which we had come to see, dated back to 1620 and was known as the 'Sistine Chapel of Peru', which is a misnomer, since the primitive murals appeared entirely out of step with the ornate baroque altar, the lavishly decorated chapels and the statues in colonial style. I swear there was a group depicting Don Quixote on his faithful mule Rosanna. We climbed up into the organ loft to see the mighty organ with keys fashioned from human bones. The organist played for us, entirely out of tune. The greatest feat in the whole performance was his effort to work the gigantic bellows. We were surrounded by children. Finally Ruth ushered them all together in front of the church to take a photograph before we left.

Delighted with our day, we returned to Cuzco. Ruth and I lost no time, but sprinted up to La Blas. Third time lucky - we found it open and were able to see the magnificent pulpit carved by a Mestizo, showing the flowing design of fruits and flowers, so very characteristic of their style. Having achieved our goal, we walked slowly down the steep narrow alleyway called San Blas. It took but little persuasion to get Ruth to step inside the small art gallery. Need I say more? We bought a lovely portrait of an Indian woman: a startling face, but the eyes were 'dead', as so many we had seen in real life.

We succumbed at last and bought a pair of Indian dolls. One of them was a replica of a woman with a spindle in her hand and a baby on her back. We also purchased some attractive etchings and intended to get some more, but there was no more time before we left Cuzco next morning.

We were sorry to leave this lovely mountain town, where we had been inordinately happy. Circling over Cuzco, we had a perfect view of the Andes before heading south on our short flight to Arequipa, where we changed planes. The heat struck up from the tarmac as we descended. Two members of our party, who were not well enough to proceed, were left behind in Arequipa.

We boarded our plane for Juliaca, which lies south of Cuzco, at a height of 3,825 metres. We knew we had a tight schedule awaiting us. Initially we were supposed to stay two nights in Juliaca, which would have given us ample time to explore Lake Titicaca and the town. However, we arrived on Friday and there were no flights back to Arequipa on Sunday, therefore we had to be satisfied with just one day.

Taxis were waiting for us at the airport. Our luggage was soon stowed away in the boots of the cars, and we piled in ourselves to travel swiftly through sun-drenched flat countryside to Juliaca. I

Floating island of the Urus Indians (Lake Titicaca).

cannot really say much about this town, since our hotel stood at the outskirts and we only caught a glimpse of the square and church in passing. A market was in full swing in the square - in fact there were many street markets all over town.

Our luggage was unloaded at the hotel and we continued our journey to the lake. We had seen its blue waters from the air before we landed. Lake Titicaca, which lies on the Peruvian-Bolivian border, is the highest navigable lake in the world. We saw mountains in the distance which were already in Bolivian territory. We reached Puno, the town on the lake itself. It struck me as an extraordinary place. Each building, built of red adobe brick, was covered by a corrugated iron roof. It must have been intensely hot during the day and bitterly cold after sunset, since the temperature dropped rapidly.

When we arrived the roofs shimmered like silver in the fierce light. We did not stop until we reached the waterfront, where motorboats were waiting for us. Once settled in two boats, we shared our picnic lunch once again. The crew of two men gladly accepted our stale bread. We sailed past an enormous building set in the rocks, apparently a hotel, which looked entirely deserted. We sailed through a strait between reeds and watched birds basking in the sun. Suddenly, roofs appeared above the reeds and soon we landed on the floating islands of the Urus Indians. These are reed islands, on which the Urus Indians have lived for many centuries. Many of them never set foot on firm land. They live off salmon fishing in the lake and eat the tutora plant which grows on the island. In fact, the islands were made of this plant. They also use tutora to build their boats.

Unfortunately, the island we visited was very much geared for tourists. The women sat on the ground offering very attractive, colourful embroidery, weaving and pottery for sale. Children, like little leeches, were clinging to us trying to sell their drawings. There was a schoolhouse on the island, set up by the Seventh-Day Adventists, who were extremely active in this area, and had adopted the Urus Indians. None of us felt at ease on this island; we left to try another one, but did not fare any better. We returned to dry land.

After tea and cake in a small bar, we continued our journey following the lake for a little while. Finally we turned off, driving inland over a hilly road to a smaller lake, Lake Umano. The light was fading as we walked up the steep slope to the extraordinary necropolis of Sillustan. Here, on a hilly terrain overlooking the lake, miles away from civilisation are chullpas, the funeral towers of pre-Colombian times. These strange structures, which were under reconstruction, housed numerous mummy bundles within their central cores, each in its own niche, resembling a beehive. A small opening at the bottom gave access to a spiral corridor to facilitate ancestor worship. Some of the towers had beautiful facing in parts and many showed traces of carvings, usually of snakes. Apart from funeral towers, there were also many subterranean galleries throughout this area. Unfortunately we had no chance to explore these. We were looking for a square temple, but failed to find it. We saw the sun set over the waters of the lake and by the time we returned to the waiting cars, darkness had descended.

It had been a most exciting day. When we reached our hotel, we found a message waiting, to inform us that we had to be at the airport at 8 am, which gave us no time at all to see Juliaca itself. We suddenly felt tired and cold. The rather dilapidated tourist hotel provided little comfort. We managed with some difficulty to obtain electric fires for our bedrooms. These had been provided in Cuzco, where they had been very welcome at times. Having changed and warmed up, we had a most hilarious meal, which we shared with Beatrice. Foolishly, I had tasted too many tit-bits from my fellow diners, so I felt unwell the next day.

Next morning we walked a little way towards town, but it was too early in the day for much activity and we were too far out of town to go on foot into the centre. We returned to our hotel and watched two women, who had already taken up position outside the hotel entrance, offering their wares. Somebody always buys.

We arrived at the airport at the appointed time, only to be told that the plane was full. An Italian party had taken precedence and we would have to wait for the self-same plane to return from Arequipa. It was a hot and sunny day. We settled down on the grassy verge. This airport had no tarmac, only simple landing strips, reminiscent of Ethiopia.

Finally the plane returned and we were actually the first to board, which was fortunate since we did not get seat tickets. We managed to get window seats and glanced down on the blue waters of Lake Titicaca before turning towards Arequipa. This again is an oasis town. We had a wonderful view of the surrounding desert, whose sand was heaped up into grotesque shapes. We saw the snow-capped cone of the volcano Elmisti (58,443 metres high), flanked on one side by Chanchani (6,096 metres) and Pichu-Pichu (5,668 metres) on the other. These three mountains, rising clear and majestic into the blue sky, were a never-ending joy and wonder to see during the next few days.

We had liked the 'feel' of Arequipa when we had briefly landed on our way to Juliaca, and were not to be disappointed. We felt happy in this 'white city'. Many of its buildings had been built of white volcanic stone called sillian. We had seen streaks of it from the air, shining brilliantly in the bright sun, contrasting with the surrounding bare mountains. Arequipa lies on the earthquake belt and therefore houses are only one storey high. In fact, the new hotel, Hotel President, sticks out like a sore thumb with its many storeys. Arequipa is the third largest town in Peru, almost entirely Spanish, in contrast to Cuzco.

We drove from the airport through sunny streets to our hotel. The pleasant Tourist Hotel in warm orange colour, stood above, opposite a lively park much used by families on Sundays and holidays. We were assured that the centre of town was within easy walking distance. The hotel was pleasantly cool with spacious reception rooms and a garden with swimming pool. Sadly, the last earthquake, which occurred on 15th of February this year, had cracked the swimming pool and it was therefore empty. Behind it, at the end of the garden, lived an enormous tortoise, which responded to gentle stroking of its forefoot, poking its head out of its shell cautiously. If you stroked its neck with tender care, it raised its head towards the sun. Having completed our preliminary tour of inspection, we unpacked and settled into our comfortable rooms.

Before leaving London we had been asked by a Peruvian friend of a friend of mine to deliver two small packages to her aunts. One in Lima, the other in Arequipa. The first had been collected from our hotel in Lima, following a telephone call made on our behalf by the hotel manager. We neither saw the lady, nor did she leave a message. Maria, the niece, had told us that her aunt in Arequipa lived near the Tourist Hotel. Siesta over, we sallied forth, crossed the cool grassy square and, after asking once or twice, found ourselves outside a pleasant villa. A maid answered our ring and hastily withdrew, clutching the small parcel and Maria's letter to her bosom. Shortly afterwards, the lady of the house opened the door and welcomed us, obviously delighted to see us, and ushered us inside. Her English was limited and we did not speak Spanish. We sat and talked and were offered iced Inca Cola. Finally we set off for town.

Arequipa is easy to get to know, since as with all other Spanish towns, it is laid out in a grid system. By now, we automatically made for the Plaza de Armas. But on our way, Signora Julia took us to the former Jesuit cloisters adjacent to the church of La Compania. It no longer served as cloisters: small shops, boutiques and art galleries occupied the former cells beneath cool arches, blending in tastefully with the elegant architecture. There were three courtyards. The first was most elaborate with beautiful carvings on graceful columns and arches. The remaining two were simpler, but conveyed a greater sense of tranquility. The whole complex was very Moorish in style. Pure enchantment, particularly in the fading light.

Our next visit was to La Compania, which had a most elaborately carved facade and was extremely ornate inside. The most amazing sight was the royal chapel, which was entirely covered by beautifully preserved murals. There were some lovely paintings and carved figures of the saints and a most extraordinary font, flanked on either side by columns (which were really legs terminating in heads instead of feet). Very Indian in concept and entirely pre-Christian in style.

We reached the flowered Plaza de Armas and saw the twin-towered cathedral bathed in the golden light of the setting sun, with the snow-capped cone of El Misti behind it. The cathedral occupied one entire side of the square. The remaining three sides were faced by colonial buildings with shady arcades.

Our kind guide took us into a few shops. Most of these were extremely elegant and had some exquisite handmade articles for sale. We passed the church of San Augustine, also with the typical Andean Mestizo facade, but as time was running out, we returned to our hotel. We said goodbye to Signorina Julia, hoping that we would see her again. In fact, she intended to give us a letter for her niece, but it remained our first and last encounter. We enquired in vain at the desk in our hotel whether a message had been left for us.

One member of our party, Nina, a Russian-born eye surgeon, had been installed in the bridal suite, consisting of a double bedroom, an opulent bathroom fitted with bath and bidet and a well-appointed, most elegant sitting room. It seemed a pity to waste this setting, so she decided to have a bottle party before dinner. Since everybody had bought a bottle at London Airport on the way out, we all were able to contribute. Gordon, a retired schoolteacher, provided nuts and roasted beans (which were a speciality of Peru). He had also ordered fresh orange juice from the hotel. This spontaneous party was a most pleasant interlude.

The sun stood brilliantly in the blue sky next morning and to our joy, we could have our breakfast on the terrace, overlooking the town. We set off on foot, crossing the little park in front of the hotel. We descended steep, narrow lanes, which took us through San La Dar, the oldest part of Arequipa. We reached Santa Catalina, which in fact is a town with a town, surrounded by city walls. It was originally founded by a Spanish noblewoman, a widow, and her daughter in the 16th century. In those far-off days, only Spanish women and girls of substance were allowed to enter the order. Their parents had to supply a dowry, sufficient to provide for a house with two rooms and a kitchen, suitably furnished, and to procure a serving girl. One report stated that there were 450 nuns living in total seclusion with 200 unpaid servants. But the reports regarding the exact numbers varied. The few nuns who remained had retreated into a new monastery within the walls. The rest of Santa Catalina has been opened to the public. All streets were named after towns in Spain. There was the enchanting Toledo Street with buttresses adorned with flower pots, Calle Burgos, Granada, etc.

We first entered the nuns' sitting room, well furnished with carpets and comfortable chairs. Here they sang and chatted whilst they sewed. We saw the communal kitchen, formerly a church, with pots and pans, ovens and enormous storage jars.

We walked in and out of nuns' houses, large and small, according to their means, with alcoves containing their beds. One enterprising lady even had a water-closet, whilst all the others used their chamber pots, which were emptied into a communal sewer. The same progressive nun also had a chimney in her kitchen.

We were shown the house of the 'Bolivian Nun', who was shortly to be canonised. She had walked on foot from her native land to enter the convent against her parents' wishes. She was almost blind in her old age and died when she was 82. She had performed a great many good deeds and the story has it that she accomplished miracles.

We walked through the main cloister and admired the view of the trio of El Misti, Chan-Chani and Pichu-Pichu, framed by the bright little houses. We stopped at the refectory for tea and delicious home-made cakes before continuing our journey through this place of pure enchantment with its maze of cobbled streets, flower-decked cloisters and buttressed houses in vivid colours of blue, red and orange. Blue stood for purification, red for life in the convent, and orange for the life thereafter.

We walked along the Calle Cordoba, followed the Calle Toledo, which led us to the laundry. A very ingenious place. The water ran in a central channel from a spring and then flowed into enormous storage jars, which had been halved, forming large basins to either side.

Each of the nuns' houses used to have a staircase leading up to the flat roof. There they could dry their washing and also sunbathe undisturbed.

It had been a splendid morning. We spent our siesta in the comfort of the hotel garden, which was pleasant even with an empty pool. We had shared our lunch with Beatrice and her room-mate and decided to explore the town together. We started off as a foursome, heading for San Camilo, the Indian market. This was fascinating, as were all markets. Everything you wanted was here to buy, from underwear to food. Amidst all the squalor and confusion, we discovered a proper old-fashioned clown entertaining his audience, who were spellbound. We also saw a number of trestle tables standing in a row, where people, oblivious to all the hubbub around them, were engrossed in playing chess and another boardgame. We had seen these games played in some of the public squares in Lima.

Soon we lost our companions, since we had stopped to buy some shoes for Ruth, whose walking shoes were slowly falling apart. Having been successful, we consulted our map and decided to make for La Merced. We passed a few stragglers of the market vendors, sitting on the dirty pavements selling half-rotten fruit. La Merced, when we arrived, was firmly closed. We asked a passing clergyman and he indicated that the church would open at 6 pm.

We had made our way towards the Plaza de Armas and stopped to rest and have a cup of coffee in one of the small bars under the cool arcades which surrounded the square. It was Sunday afternoon and all the world had come out into the sun.

We slipped into the cathedral, which was packed to overflowing for the service, which was drawing to a close. Rebuilt in the 19th century, this cathedral is very simple, almost austere, compared with all the other churches in Arequipa. We returned to La Merced, which was open. It had a lovely statue of the Virgin above the side portal, an ornate altar, the usual profusion of carvings and many statues of saints and paintings, all of which we had come to know so well in the churches of Arequipa and in all other places we had visited.

We returned to our hotel and once again had a party in Nina's reception room before dinner.

I was up early the next day and had a splendid time walking on my own through the streets, admiring the fine colonial buildings. I stepped into the little church of San La Zaro and into the cool atmosphere of Santa Catalina. In the latter I found that all altars, except the main one, had been covered by purple cloth. I walked for miles and found the pretty little church of Santa Rosa, before returning for my breakfast, which we had once again out on the terrace in brilliant sunshine.

We set off by coach, this time to visit the imposing church of San Francisco, which stood on a square next to the Founder's House - a fine colonial building converted to an artshop and museum. The church itself consisted of two parts, an older, simple chapel and a newer, more ornate one. Some of our group followed our local guide to see the tranquil cloisters with their treasures of paintings and statues. The statues of San Francisco and of San Domingo stood side by side. On their respective birthdays they are carried through the town in solemn procession to their own convent to celebrate the day in style with a proper birthday party, bowing to each other in brotherly greetings.

I quickly looked into the museum. Apart from the usual numerous paintings, one room was given over entirely to prints of agriculture through the ages. Arequipa had been an important city in the times of the Incas.

We drove to two suburbs of the town. Yaha Huane had a pleasant Plaza de Armas, lying high above Arequipa, presenting a fine view of the city shimmering in bright sunshine. Once gain, the church on the Plaza had an elaborately carved facade, which had been carved in dazzling sillian with a profusion of plants. Incorporated into the design was an Indian face side by side with Christian symbols.

Cayma, high above the town, with an attractive cobbled street, was festooned with geraniums. The sun streamed down, and an old lady greeted us from behind the grill of her window. We felt as if we had suddenly been transported to Seville.

Each section of Arequipa had its own Plaza de Armas. These were most attractive - regardless whether they were in an old part or in a new development the Plaza remained an important focal point in the life of the people.

Our guide was a softly spoken young man, who did not hail from Arequipa. His parents were wealthy; he was a student. Some of his ancestors had come from Russia. He told us that Arequipa had the highest living standard in Peru and that people here were proud of their Spanish descent. Old established English families, such as the Ricketts and Fawcetts, were immensely rich and lived on

La Compania de Jesu (Arequipa).

Petroglyps.

beautiful estates. Arequipa was a busy commercial centre and also the centre for dairy products. Milk was being handled by the American firm of Carnation. We passed their enormous plant on our way out of town, driving along the river Chilli. We admired the well-preserved irrigation canal running along the river, still from Inca times. Once again the desert extended into the fertile Chilli valley, where grass was cultivated for cattle fodder and where onions were planted for export, mainly to Japan. Incidentally, Arequipa beer was being shipped across the ocean to Switzerland. Behind the hill, called Green Hill, lay the biggest copper mine in the world.

We had left the elegant city behind, had driven through the fertile Chilli valley and had arrived at the 'Pueblo Nouves'. These are mean shacks, hovels, which Indian immigrants had put up on the barren desert ground around Arequipa. According to our guide, out of 150,000 only 2,000 pay tax - the rest do not qualify, since they do not earn enough. Vast numbers of Indians streamed into Arequipa each day. Indians had never been slaves in name, but because they could not pay their taxes, they had to work the copper mines. They became unfit to either work hard or perform skilled labour. In 1850 a large Chinese immigration took place. These immigrants were put to building the railway. The biggest Chinese quarter in the whole of South America existed in Lima. There were certainly many Chinese restaurants in Lima, called Chifa, where food was simple and cheap. Strange to relate, a large irrigation scheme was being planned by six nations and Britain was one of the participants. But they had to import labour, this time from South Africa. Completion of this project was planned for 1983. Arequipa drew its precious water from the snow-capped mountains and stored it in large reservoirs.

We left this heart-breaking site of human misery behind us and drove to a small oasis with a beautifully restored mill. The contrast between the stark poverty of 'Pueblo Nouves' and the Sabandia Mill was almost too much to bear.

Deep in thought, we returned to town. Many of our party decided to spend the rest of the day at the swimming pool of a private club. We returned to our hotel to rest in the garden and shared our lunch with two men, who were cleaning some awnings. After our siesta, we went to town once more to savour the special atmosphere of the place and to do some last-minute shopping, during the course of which we kept on meeting members of our party. We found some most elegant shops tucked away in arcades and located a number of craftshops in a small alleyway behind the cathedral, where we met a young English woman whose husband was involved in the irrigation scheme. With her help we found a leather shop, where we bought a pouffe. Finally Ruth found some beautifully soft, 100% alpaca wool. Satisfied with our purchases we returned to our hotel to join once more in the fun of a final party. This time we had soft drinks and excellent cakes. An odd choice before dinner, but we all enjoyed it.

Rumour had it that there was an Englishman in Arequipa who organised special tours up canyons and other exciting places in his ancient Landrover, provided she did not break down. This sounded so tempting that we tried to persuade others to join us in this adventure. We tried to make up a party of six but, although initially most had been enthusiastic, all bar three backed out. The five of us decided on a trip next morning, hoping to return by midday, to join our group for the flight to Lima. This Englishman appeared at our final party complete with poor photographs demonstrating some of the sights to be seen. He assured us that he had once more repaired his 'motor' and all would be well. We arranged to meet at 4.30 am the next day. Elated by the prospect of an adventure, we dined in high spirits and packed our belongings. Somehow we found it easy to rise at 4 am, though of course it was still dark. At 4.30 we left - Ruth, myself, Bob, an extremely nice man from Cambridge (he dealt in agricultural machines), Neville, an odd architect from Liverpool, and Georgina, a white-haired widow from Nottingham, a retired teacher. We travelled south and somehow during our journey into the unknown we became a close-knit unit for a short time. We sped through the sleeping town. Now and again the velvet silence was shattered by the loud barking of dogs. We began to climb, leaving Arequipa behind. Travelling speedily on an excellent road, we met a good deal of traffic, mostly lorries coming towards Arequipa.

It was getting lighter. I was watching for the sun to rise when, on a steep incline, we drew to a sudden halt. Something was wrong with the car. Apparently a Landrover has both an overdrive as well as an ordinary one. The first is necessary to negotiate difficult terrain. This had become impacted. Fortunately we had two able-bodied men with us, who knew the inside of machines. Georgina and I left them to it and meandered along the road. It was too cold to stand and stare. The sun rose behind the bare mountains and illuminated the desolate scene of rock and sand. Three quarters of an hour later, we were on our way again, gently climbing to reach a high plateau with the most amazing grey sand dunes, quite unique in appearance and formation. All were crescent shaped and of varying size, from 6 to 30 metres across, and from 2 to 5 metres high. All of them stood in orderly rows behind each other with their pointed ends looking leewards. These sand dunes moved 15 metres along each year.

We came to yet another unforeseen halt. We stopped at one of the rare petrol stations along the wayside to fill up the tank and to check the tyre pressure, only to find that one had a puncture. There was precious little tread left on any of them. No matter, Mr. H. changed the wheel, whilst we stretched our legs once again. He left the punctured tyre behind to be repaired. Not only did he leave the tyre, but he also - by oversight - left his pressure gauge, which could not be found when we returned later to collect the mended tyre. Nor could he find his guiding licence, which he had already dropped twice out of his top pocket when he bent down to find a stone to place beneath the wheel on our first stop! Fortunately he did find his licence, safely tucked in his toolbox after he had left us, together with a sizeable dollar bill. Poor Mr. H. was not very efficient to say the least, but full of grand ideas. He was actually part Peruvian: his father was Peruvian, his mother English. He had returned to Peru with his English wife 25 years ago, to make his fortune. Luckily, his wife kept the homefires burning by working as a secretary at the Carnation factory, whilst Mr. H. continued to struggle along, hoping to strike lucky in the end. His poor Landrover was 14 years old and on its last legs, but by the time Mr. H. had paid for the repairs, there was no money left to buy a new one, unless he could have found a generous backer.

We set off again, driving through varied scenery of large craggy mountains, fertile valleys, passing small hamlets. We drove up and down gradients at a steady speed. Some mountain ridges were perfectly flat, as if a hand had levelled them with a spirit level; others were heaped up into pleats and folds. They were mostly grey in colour, but occasionally clear greens and reds appeared. The hamlets themselves always stood on barren ground, adjacent to well-cultivated lush oases. Quite obviously, fertile land was far too precious to be used as building plots.

We had reached a high point: 300 ft below us lay the Majes Valley. We dropped down slowly into it and crossed the river to stop at Punta Colorado, the 'Rose Coloured Village', which was aptly named, nestling beneath a rose-coloured cliff. We had been delayed once more on our way, since we had to wait until an earth remover had cleared the way following a recent landslide. We were in fact near the centre of the recent earthquake. We had breakfast at Punta Colorado, consisting of delicious steaming hot herb tea, presented in an enormous enamel cup, accompanied by two fresh rolls, all for the equivalent sum of five English pennies. We enjoyed our breakfast, sitting in a mud hut at a table covered with an oilcloth, watched by many eager childrens' faces crowding round the entrance of the 'restaurant'. There were neither doors nor glass in the windows, just open apertures. Refreshed and ready to continued we picked up a dirt track, passed sugar canes and fields of maize until all vegetation suddenly stopped. We had arrived at Toro Muerto of the lower canyon. We walked up the steep hill. Sinking deeply into the soft sand, we came upon the most amazing sight: a vast desert area was strewn with many rocks of all shapes and sizes with most of them bearing fascinating petroglyphs. Up to date, about 400 have been found. Two years ago two German geologists had worked here for two weeks photographing, cataloguing and sampling. There may be a publication in the pipeline. All we were told was that these intriguing carvings had been executed by an unknown Indian tribe some 1,000 years ago. Some were easy to decipher. No end of llamas were in evidence. The sun appeared again and again. The snake, the puma, the condor were all well represented. Men, and in one instance a woman, could be seen. Some petroglyphs however were very puzzling indeed. It was a tremendous and unique experience, almost the highlight of the whole journey.

We made good time on our way back, although we had to stop to collect the tyre, and halted again to look in vain for Mr. H.'s guide licence.

We reached the hotel in time to have a snack, before leaving for the airport with the inevitable waiting period for our flight to Lima. The small airport was packed with excited crowds, who sang lustily. Finally everyone, ourselves included, was presented with a leaflet. Evidently 'Billy Graham of Peru' was about to arrive at Arequipa. We saw the plane arrive, but the crowd surged forwards and we never saw the man.

After a short flight to Lima over vast areas of absolute desert we quickly boarded a waiting coach and drove through parts of the town which we had not seen before, with most elegant villas set in well-cared for gardens in tree-lined avenues. Most windows in these low buildings had very attractive ornamental wrought-iron grills across them. Whether these were meant purely as decoration or were actually primarily used for security remained open for conjecture.

Our journey was a long one over bumpy roads with a very bad-tempered driver, who drove most erratically. Usually the cars we had driven in, however dilapidated, just purred along and most drivers had been quite excellent. It was completely dark by the time we left Lima to take the Pan American Highway along the coast northwards to Paracas. Ruth and I, well satisfied with our day, dozed on and off and would have happily foregone food and drink to get to bed. We reached Hotel Paracas at 11.30 pm, 150 km north of Lima. Not only had a three-course meal been prepared for all of us, but a glass of pisco sour awaited us.

Paracas was the last place where we stayed. The hotel stood in the bay of the same name, on the site of the original archaeological camp. The nearest habitation was the Port of Pisco, fifteen kilometres south. The main building had a conference room, which housed a fine collection of local ceramics, collected by an Englishman. Double bedrooms with showers attached occupied small bungalows connected by archways. Each 'little house' had its own porch with table and bench. There was a swimming pool, tennis court and clock golf to amuse the guests. All looked elegant and expensive.

The whole surrounding area, the entire peninsula of Paracas, is a vast necropolis of a civilisation which flourished 1,000 years ago. But there were more attractions in store for us.

We were up early next morning, waiting at the jetty to board a rowing boat, which took us out to a motor boat to sail to the Ballesha Islands, which are most strange in their rock formations, with natural grottos and arches, covered by birds. For centuries, the Indians used to mine guano, the bird droppings, to use as fertiliser. We still saw the evidence of ancient mines.

I have never seen such a vast number and great variety of birds. I can only name a few of them: the brown pelican, the condor, the penguin and various gulls. The birds shared the rocks with hundreds of sea lions. Big ones and small ones, they were in and out of the water. They jumped gracefully out of the ocean or waddled clumsily up the sunny rocks. They made the most deafening noise. Around the boat floated the colourful octopus, pink, yellow, green, with flowing tentacles. It certainly was an experience not to be missed. Skimming along the coastline, which was being developed into a nature reserve, we were suddenly confronted by the curious tracing of the candelabra. No one knows who carved this huge edifice into the barren hillside, nor does anyone know what it means. It was very striking, seen from the ocean. The water here, thanks to the warm Humbolt current, was teeming with fish. It is impossible to escape the smell of fishmeal along the whole of the coastline. Fishmeal is processed in this region and forms one of the most important export goods Peru has to offer the world.

Far in the distance rose a modern monument dramatically out of the sand dunes. This marked the spot where San Martin, the black saint, was said to have first set foot on Peruvian soil.

Our journey back from the islands was rather choppy and we were happy to reach dry land and rest at the poolside for a little while.

Nearby was an old Inca ruin called Tambo Colorado, which could be reached by taxi or bus. Taxis were not available on that afternoon, but it so happened that an international archaeological conference was based at the hotel and they had planned to visit Tambo Colorado in an Unesco bus that same afternoon. Three of us asked whether we could join in and were invited to take the backseats. Most of the archaeologists were from South America and, according to their custom, did not rise from their midday siesta until after 3 pm. The bus was full. We sat quietly and very discreetly on the last seats. We got as far as Pisco, where we stopped to fill up with petrol. The guide announced that it was far too late to reach Tambo Colorado by daylight. He suggested a visit to the local museum instead. The bus returned to the hotel to drop those who did not wish to visit the museum, but we sat tight and travelled along the peninsular through vast areas of nothingness. Where formerly temples and cities had stood, now there was only sand. The museum was small but very attractively laid out, with ceramics, textiles, some implements and a reconstructed burial ground as well as reconstructed living quarters.

The party decided to continue up to the headland to see the sea lions. We continued through sand and more sand to a tiny fishing village where these jolly people bought fish and Inca Cola before driving on. The bus stopped finally in the middle of nowhere and we all staggered over sand and rock to the top of the cliffs to listen to the roar of the sea lions. By then it was too dark to see them. We all made our way back to the bus, which was quite hazardous over the uneven terrain in the pitch dark. It did not occur to the driver to switch on the headlights of the bus to guide us safely back. Hilarity ruled on the return journey. I talked to a young woman from Chile, formerly a lawyer, now an archaeologist in Chicago, and to a nice young man, an anthropologist from Equador. We all agreed that the furtive afternoon trip had been great fun.

Our adventure into the past was not yet over. Next morning we set off on a long taxi ride. We left the coast, heading inland across desert to the oasis town of Ica. This actually was the centre of the wine-growing area of Peru. As we were nearing the town, the roadside was lined with stalls offering grapes, mangoes, melons and other fruit as well as wines and their brandy, known as Pisco, after the seaport. We had to stop, as always, when passing from one department to another, for the driver to have his papers checked. We decided to get some fruit on our way back. Occasionally a toll was demanded for cars. We had had to do this on our trip with Mr. H. to the petroglyphs, and again on our way to Nazca from Ica.

The countryside we travelled through was most forbidding and inhospitable, although from time to time attempts had been made, somewhat feebly, to cultivate the land. It had been fertile in Inca times, due to intensive irrigation. We could still see traces of their canals, now dry and overgrown. Apparently the water tables had dropped and the consumption of water had increased throughout the country.

We reached a high plateau and passed the observation tower, from which it was possible to see two of the Nazca designs. We drove through the little town of Nazca out to the airport, where we had to wait our turn to take one of the small crafts, which had only room for three. Some of us elected to go back to Nazca to visit the small museum. This consisted of only one room, but displayed beautiful ceramics. The Nazcan civilisation reached its peak about 800 AD. Apart from the exquisitely decorated ceramic, there were wooden carvings and lovely woven materials. Intricately woven bands were used as headbands right through pre-Inca times and later in the Inca period. They had a tassel in the centre. The ancient designs were still being used by the women in Cuzco and the tourists bought them to use as belts, bellropes or simply as ornamental hangings.

We strolled across the sun-drenched Plaza de Armas. I slipped into the modern church. We took a quick walk through the market, where an old woman deftly ground corn between two stones. Time had come for us to return for our flight. We climbed aboard the small craft and flew across the large area, 22 km away from Nazca, stretching on either side of the Pan American Highway, as the pilot explained, as he dipped precariously to the right and now to the left, swooping and looping, carried away by his enthusiasm. Poor Honor, sitting next to him, was sick and silly little Mr. Brown, next to me, could neither understand the pilot nor see what there was to see - he really had no idea what it was all about. As far as I know, these mysterious lines and shapes had only been discovered fairly recently.

Some tracings were easily recognisable, such as the monkey, a whale, a fish, spider, tree and a spiral. But there were also trapezoidal shapes, looking like landing pads. No one had solved the mystery. All tracings were of such enormous size that they could only be fully appreciated from the air.

We landed, somewhat green around the gills. It was very hot. There was no sign of our taxi drivers, who had either gone for lunch or found some shade for their siesta. Not everyone had journeyed to Nazca; some had elected to stay in Ica and meet us there. We all met eventually on the Plaza de Armas of this bustling little town. We just had time to snatch a sandwich before we hastily followed the rest in search of the museum. It had been moved out of town. We drove to the new building, which was most pleasantly set out and was classed as one of the best in Peru. We only visited the ground floor, which contained artifacts from pre-Inca times up to the Inca period. Upstairs were very interesting maps and plans, appertaining to all archaeological sites in Peru. Unfortunately, the day was drawing to an end and we had to return to Paracas. We stopped on our way, as planned, to buy fruit for our next day's journey back to Lima.

The last morning dawned. I had a swim in the pool before breakfast. We had sufficient time to sit by the pool for a while where I - incidentally or accidentally - got involved, at this late stage, with one of our fellow travellers, who saw fit to 'pour out his heart'.

For once, we lunched in style in the restaurant of Paracas Hotel, before setting off. This time we did not doze off, but kept alert, watching the scenery, which was at times quite spectacular, glide past. Lush green oases, cotton fields as we had seen in other parts, gave way to deserts, where sand spirals rose into the air. Suddenly, in nowhere, we passed chicken factories. We saw and smelt the sea.

After a couple of hours we stopped to stretch our legs. Once again stalls, selling fruit and wine, stood by the wayside. We purchased two bottles of Pisco to take home. Maybe one day I shall try to make pisco sour for my friends.

We had been promised one more visit to an ancient site, before finally returning to Lima. Encircling the crest of a hill, 20 kilometres north of the city, lay the ruins of Pachacamac in the Lurin Valley. This had been the largest coastal town at the time of the Spaniards' arrival in Peru. We left the road to climb up to a pretty small museum, set in the midst of a lush garden. The contrast between this well-cared for garden and the desert around us was quite striking.

Hernando Pizzaro, the brother of the leader, was the first European to come to Pachacamac and in 1533 he destroyed the idols, killed the priests, looted the temples, but failed to find the gold and treasures he had expected. The tortured priests remained adamant that all gold had been despatched northwards at the Inca's request. Whether they spoke the truth and it had formed part of the last Inca's ransom, now all melted down, or whether a large treasure still lies hidden in the Andes, no one knows.

We drove up to the ruins of the temple, which used to be crowned by the Temple of the Sun. It was a most impressive complex, with terraces, steps, walls, niches, corridors; but the stonework was quite crude. It might have been constructed in a great hurry. We looked from these heights down to the Lurin Valley and across the sea, where the sun was sinking, and on the other side, to the hills where we could still see the ruins of the mighty city that was Pachacamac.

We briefly looked down into the Temple of the Virgins with its many rooms and courtyards, its bath and cisterns. We admired the noble bust of Dr. Julio Tello, the father of Peruvian archaeology, framed on either side by tall cacti, before boarding the bus to drive back to Lima.

In Lima we had one hour to spare before meeting up with our party for a final festive meal. We wandered towards the Plaza de Armas and strolled down the bustling Union Street. All street vendors were out and business was brisk. We did our last-minute shopping. Crossing the Plaza de Armas on our way back, we saw a gun carrier and a large number of soldiers. We wondered, but paid little heed. We were quickly diverted by a nuptial mass in one of the chapels of the cathedral. We also saw that another wedding was taking place in the church of San Francisco, but had no time to stop and stare. As pre-arranged, we met our party in a pleasant restaurant, a former colonial house with spacious courtyard and lofty rooms. The rest of our group had fared badly. Apparently they had been caught up in a student demonstration. A Communist-inspired revolt, so we were told. All tourists were pulled into various shops, the shutters came down, the doors were locked. Some people were advised to take off all jewellery and watches. Ladies on their own were escorted to our meeting place by taxi. This of course explained the presence of the gun carrier and soldiers in the Plaza. Sad as it was, we were not surprised, since we had seen many slogans daubed on walls and buildings, which had disturbed us and had made us realise that all was not well in Peru. However, a pisco sour, followed by an excellent meal, blotted out the fear experienced by so many. Soon time had come to drive to the airport.

Lima Airport was full to the brim and we were calmly told that there was no room on the plane for us. We waited patiently, standing around, or sitting on the floor. Finally they let us on board. We hurriedly handled our luggage ourselves and climbed on board. We left Lima two hours behind schedule.

We landed in Ecuador as before and took on more passengers. Miami was our next stop. We all had to leave the plane. All luggage had to be unlocked, and although we were only in transit, we had to submit to stringent customs and passport checks. We arrived two hours late at Kennedy Airport.

We spent a pleasant day in New Rochelle with my niece and family. We indulged in the luxury of a hot bath and changed from tropical kit into warm clothes.

It was soon time to return to the airport. We were again two hours late leaving. Tired from our long journey, we fell asleep on the plane and slept fitfully until we woke to see the sun rise over the ocean.

We had a lift back to our flat. Exhausted, we went straight to bed and slept soundly, waking later refreshed and able to face the daily grind after our exciting time.